A Specimen
Fishing Year

A
Specimen
Fishing
Year

JOHN WILSON'S FISHING DIARY

ADAM & CHARLES BLACK · LONDON

© 1977 JOHN WILSON

First published 1977
A. & C. Black Ltd.
35 Bedford Row, London WC1R 4JH

ISBN 0 7136 1799 3

Typeset by Computacomp (UK) Ltd., Fort William, Scotland
and printed by Page Bros (Norwich) Ltd., Norwich

Dedication

To my wife, Barbara, without
whose tolerance my fishing
would most certainly suffer.

Contents

INTRODUCTION

My interest in catching specimen fish stemmed from my early fishing days when, at the tender age of thirteen, I joined the Enfield Town Angling Club in North London. The club ran regular monthly coach outings to more exciting places than the nearby river Lea, though it held some good fish and still does despite water abstraction. But my technique at the time was sadly lacking in expertise.

Several older members of the club took us youngsters under their wing, and one of them — Denis Brown, a fine angler — taught me the basics of size-limit match fishing, how to read different swims, to avoid catching the dreaded bleak, and how to tackle up. He taught me how to use a roach pole on the Thames, and the intricacies of presenting hempseed while baiting with elderberrys, tares or casters (chrysalids in those days). Denis was a past master at catching 'goers' — fish which exceeded the Thames size limits. Only these (such as roach over eight inches, bream over twelve inches, etc) were eligible for weighing-in on club outings.

In size-limit fishing it is truly amazing just how many $7^1/_2$-inch roach and $11^1/_2$-inch bream there are. I often caught quite good bags of undersized fish on our outings to the Great Ouse, the Kennet and the Thames. But it took several trips before I actually weighed in. I realised then that bigger fish were not only more difficult to catch but also more interesting.

Denis showed me that by fishing close to, or actually on, the bottom — was the way to lure the goers. He taught me how to lower the plummet quietly into the swim at the end of the pole, and then adjust the float (a short length of peacock quill — still my favourite float material) so that it lay half-cocked. It was easy for me to imagine what the quill would do when a fish mouthed the bait and moved the small shot fixed just two inches from it.

I quickly learned this new technique and many others, but my real day of triumph came on a coach outing to the Old Bedford River near Mepal two years later. Everyone had expected Denis to win the stake money as usual, but at the weigh in I pipped him by catching six good roach to his five. I took them by fishing stewed wheat on weightless tackle beneath a matchstick in a small hole in the weeds. When Denis came over to congratulate me after the weigh-in and asked me how I caught them I knew I had arrived.

I was a regular weekly companion of Denis from that moment on. We fished for roach in the London reservoirs where Denis had tried for years to catch a two pounder. I weighed several for him up to 1 lb 15 oz but, sadly, I don't think he ever achieved his ambition. How I would love to take him fishing on the Wensum now. He took me chub fishing, piking, perching and taught me so much about different waters.

Then I began travelling alone, visiting the smaller rivers in Hertfordshire. My first motor bike made it possible to visit spots further from home, like the river Rib at Wadesmill near Ware. On this little river I was to learn, through much trial and error, another technique — that of presenting the freelined bait to say nothing of the art of concealment. I caught many good fish from this little river, roach to $1^3/_4$ lbs, dace to 14 oz and chub to over 2 lb all on freelined flake or cheesepaste, but I could not better a chub of 2 lbs 11 oz, and not until two years later when on holiday at Throop Mill on the Dorset Stour did I finally take a three-pounder. A four-pounder on my very next cast both blurred and highlighted the event at the same time.

It was during that same year that I first became interested in the fishing potential of Norfolk and Suffolk. A friend, Doug Pledger, and I decided that we wanted to catch a really big bream or roach and looked through *Angling Times* at the holiday advertisements. We chose to stay at the Watch House Inn, Bungay, on the river Waveney, where big roach, tench and bream were temptingly listed.

The journey was far too long for our motor bikes so we took a coach from North London to Norfolk and started a week's fishing that was the prelude to my eventually living there.

That week's holiday on the Waveney was truly glorious. Doug and I caught mountains of big roach, any one of which would have had half the anglers along the bank to see it had it been from the Lea. They were deep-bodied, bronze-coloured beauties with brilliant red fins — and they took our baits oh-so-confidently. We both caught bream over 5 lb and on the last day of our holiday I caught my first roach over 2 lb. An unforgettable moment!

For several years — as my obsession with specimen fish grew — I often made the long journey from London to Norfolk for a day's roaching. The big-fish potential coupled with the unspoilt surroundings were always worth the effort despite those inevitable blank days.

In my early twenties I started to develop a wanderlust and decided to join the Merchant Navy. My freshwater fishing was kept alive only by having angling journals posted to me each week, but I enjoyed myself catching sea fish of all shapes and sizes from sharks to sailfish all around the globe. A spell in Barbados in the West Indies after leaving the Merchant Navy added further to my sea fishing knowledge, when I was able to fish the shallow beaches at night for big stingrays and tarpon.

However, I think I knew all along that for sheer enjoyment, freshwater fishing in England was my first love. So when my family and I arrived back in Britain in 1970 we decided to live in Norfolk where I could fish regularly for my favourite species.

During these past few years I have explored much of the available fishing in Norfolk and Suffolk. Although one tends to associate these counties with the broads and the tidal rivers, there is far more potential for specimen fish in the clean-flowing upper rivers, lakes and gravel pits within the area. However, I have occasionally been fortunate enough to fish several private broads, unaffected by boats and overcrowding, where the fishing is almost as good as the whole of Broadland was two decades ago.

In those days Oulton Broad was regularly producing perch over 3 lb and held the record with a beauty of $4^3/_4$ lb. To catch a perch of any size on the broads nowadays is an event. Hickling Broad, Horsey Mere and Heigham Sounds, once the big three of Broadland, produced in the period between 1950 and 1969 pike of 40 lb perch of over 4 lb, numerous rudd over 3 lb and tench over 6 lb. Then the killer, algae prymnesium, broke out, killing everything in its path. Massive restocking was carried out after the deaths, resulting today in good numbers of bream and roach being caught — but whether the big rudd, pike and perch will ever appear in profusion again remains to be seen.

At present, the lakes, pits and the upper reaches of the Waveney, Bure, Yare and Wensum hold by far the best potential for the specimen hunter. The Wensum in particular produces fish of an exceptionally high average size and in good numbers too. Its roach are fantastic — growing to 3 lb and over. These, as you will find out, are my favourite quarry and I spend much of my winter fishing in pursuit of them.

Prior to writing this book, I had caught roach to 2 lb $9^1/_2$ oz, so I was very happy to have improved upon this whilst writing the following pages. Other personal best fish prior to this year were 6lb tench, 2 lb 2 oz perch, 19 lb pike, 5 lb $2^1/_4$ oz chub, 8 lb 5 oz bream, 1 lb 1 oz dace, and 7 lb 10 oz zander. I have enjoyed some excellent sport trying to improve upon these weights.

Without question, I must say that this year has been my best ever for catching specimens, so perhaps the reader will forgive my flippancy when writing of catching numbers of big fish (particularly roach and tench) any one of which might well be a lifetime's ambition for an angler living in an area not so rich in big fish. However, these big fish have only been caught after several years of researching different waters, and by pooling information with friends to find those waters containing large fish in profusion. It is for these reasons that I have, where necessary, given fictitious names to several of the waters I fish.

I hope that my experiences may help other anglers attracted to specimen hunting to do likewise; but most of all I hope the following diary brings to the reader all the fun, the dedication, and the heartbreak which surrounds the hunting of specimen fish.

John Wilson

A NEW YEAR

Thursday, 1 January
Sky overcast, slight SW wind, mild.

Today's piking trip turned into the type that you want to forget. At least that is how Doug Allen and I felt as we drove home, feeling frustrated that we had had nearly twenty runs but had precious little to show for our efforts.

We had decided to boat-fish a twenty-five acre natural lake near Norwich called "the Conifers". A beautiful, almost circular, deep water which is shielded from strong winds around most of its perimeter by tall, ivy covered, fir trees. Hence the name.

Thick rush beds interspersed with fallen trees cover the margins where a depth of three feet drops suddenly down to ten. The contours then ramble across the lake, varying between ten and fifteen feet deep, to the shallows on the other side.

There is usually fair visibility of three to four feet and the fish stocks are bream in plenty (though only averaging around the pound), pike averaging six to twelve pounds and masses of small roach and perch. Tench are reputed to grow large in the lake though I have yet to fish here during the summer. My first three outings in October and November of last year resulted in eight pike ranging from 5 lb to 17 lb 9 oz — all on herrings, either static float fished or drifted along the bottom.

Today, bang in the middle of a mild spell and after a week of icy weather, should have seen the pike population on the move. They were, too, but in a most peculiar way.

In addition to the herrings being drifted towards the shore from our anchorage some eighty yards out, I fished a paternostered livebait on the spare rod into the wind on the other side of the boat. About thirty minutes after our dawn start that was the first to go. I allowed a few seconds for the roach to be turned and put the hooks home, but after a strong, powerful fight lasting a couple of minutes from what was obviously a heavy double-figure pike they fell out. Not a good start, perhaps, but the next paternostered roach accounted for a plump five-pounder. Then one of Doug's herring floats slid under — a bigger one at around nine pounds. The pike in this lake like to kid themselves they are twice as big as they are and Doug had a lively tussle despite its size.

During the next hour we had another five runs all of which resulted in the pike dropping the bait or spitting it out just before netting. It was obviously one of those days when pike clamp the bait between their jaws but do not open them during the fight for the hooks to hold.

In the afternoon, after a three-hour midday lull, from three o'clock until dark we experienced a repeat performance of the morning's feeding cycle. I brought two good double-figure fish alongside the boat and both simply spat the bait out. It was useless waiting for the classic run, turning of the bait, and then striking, so on the very next take I immediately struck into the pike which, like all the afternoon fish, had grapped a wobbled herring, the statics being totally ignored. Luckily, one of the hooks found a home in the scissors and I duly boated a ten-pounder. During the last half hour Doug was on the windward side of the boat and had his small roach dead-bait picked up from the bottom no less than five times — and ejected before he could strike.

As we broke the rods down, a nasty drizzle started and we hurriedly made for the boat house without feeling any of the usual regrets that end a day's fishing.

AFTERTHOUGHT

We shall certainly give the lake another try soon, I think, concentrate more on wobbled baits or trailing large livebaits slowly against the wind if the herrings don't produce runs. I rather fancy, though, that a static deadbait is eventually going to produce a really big pike from the lake. There is certainly much room for experiment and the lake appears to hold a much larger head of reasonable pike than we had expected.

Sunday, 4 January

Very cold, slight SW wind.

Today's weather forecast told me through experience not to go roaching. However, being the eternal optimist and since I had promised Andy Jubb a day's roaching on my stretch of the river Wensum, we were on the bank at daybreak.

This particular part of the river near Ringland plays a big part in my fishing. I probably spend more time along its reedy banks in search of big roach than I do anywhere else and for two reasons. One, it is very close to home and ideally suited to spur-of-the-moment, early morning sessions before work, and two, it holds a lot of large roach. Certainly three-pounders are present; since last August I have taken nineteen over 2 lb — five from $2^1/_2$ lb to 2 lb $9^1/_2$ oz and about sixty others ranging from a pound up to 1 lb 14 oz. All have come from the same fifty-yard glide at the downstream end of the fishery, consisting of a long straight followed by a slow bend and then a short straight (flowing right to left) — my favourite swim. In all, about four hundred yards of prime roach potential between tree-lined banks some sixty feet wide.

The depth varies little, no more than five to six feet in any swim. Because of this the roach tend to roam about, so that one is never sure exactly what size fish to expect from any particular swim. However, because much of the upper Wensum is still suffering from the national roach decline of the mid-sixties, there are very few small fish about. I took a dozen small roach from 2 — 8 oz last summer but my records show that there are more fish over the pound than under. This suits the specimen roach angler of today who, paradoxically, wishes also to see more roach of all sizes to ensure a healthy future, and I believe that, although this will be a slow process, within five years much of this wonderful river will be back to its former glory.

Other inhabitants of the Wensum are an enormous head of dace (strangely, not so evident during the winter), a few perch survivors of the sixties perch decline and making a painfully slow recovery, pike in plenty — including several really good ones around twenty pounds (I took an 18 lb 14 oz fish last November) and a few brown trout — some really large. There are also a few bream, the odd hybrid, and the very occasional rudd.

Ideal winter conditions for the river are after heavy rain when the river is thickly coloured and just starting to fine down. As it runs off and the colour goes so does the feeding pattern of the roach and one is left with just a chance of a few fish during the last hour of daylight. Today, after forty eight hours of continual heavy rain, the river had a nice, thick colour and a really strong flow.

Andy and I decided to try my usual swim since he had not fished the stretch before and he settled in amongst the rushes about five yards upstream of me. We long trotted our maggot baits beneath long peacock quills needing

17

5AA shot, close to the bottom, for at least two hours without a bite and might have moved upstream where some roach were priming on the surface had not a massive roach rolled immediately opposite us.

I was of the opinion that, although few fish appeared to be present in front of us, they were big and several minutes later I had a bite which confirmed this. Unfortunately, the fish, a good one, rolled off, and so did the next. I inspected the hook to find the point was almost square. After blueing the air a little, I tied on another fine wire size 14 spade-end and resumed trotting down, but without success. Andy fared similarly and was becoming a little despondent, so we walked upriver to warm our feet and came back for another crack.

After a few swims down the sun tried to break through the heavy clouds, increasing the light values slightly. Then my float shot under. I knew immediately this was a big fish as it bored slowly upstream towards me giving a solid thump every now and then. Each time it did this I feared the hook would give, but it was well in and I eventually slid the net under my largest-ever roach — a long ($16^1/_2$ inches) beautifully conditioned fish of 2 lb $10^1/_2$ oz. Andy's face lit up, which was nothing to what mine was doing and we settled down to fishing again. Three casts later, another bite put me on my

A fine brace of roach

toes again and, although I did not expect the float to dip in the very spot where I had been catapulting maggots at the very start of the trot, despite a bow in the line the hook went home. There was something peculiar about the fight of this fish. It fought like a bream and yet had the speed of a roach. It was, of course, hybrid, riddled with black spot, and weighing 2 lb 5 oz.

Then Andy had what proved to be his only bite of the day and landed a roach of 1 lb 10 oz. Just to rub salt into the wound I hit a bite which looked like the bottom but which resulted in another superb roach of 2 lb 9 oz exactly. I was overjoyed and was ready for more but soon afterwards the sun went in and snow started to fall.

With sheer optimism we fished the rest of the day until nearly three o'clock without so much as a flicker. The snow turned to sleet and the wind changed round to a due southerly — bang in our faces. Presentation was then impossible and, cold and reluctant, we trudged back to the car.

AFTERTHOUGHT

Today taught me two things: firstly, that the bites came only during a brief spell when the suns rays penetrated the cloud enough to raise the light value a few stops. Secondly, that it is always worth going. Thanks to Andy's eagerness to fish the river, I accounted for my best roach brace; I must take him along again in better conditions.

Monday, 5 January

Mild, cloudy, no wind at all.

I could not resist rising early this morning especially after yesterday's catch. Lo and behold — the wind had dropped, increasing the temperature noticeably. I fairly raced across the meadow from the car down to the swim for an hours trotting before work. I am not sure why, but the river was actually higher than yesterday and a little more coloured. I suppose that there must be a surplus of water upriver and the mill owners are running it off.

I fished the same swim and, luckily, found the roach almost instantly on the second trot down. There appeared to be a huge shoal in the swim and I accounted for eleven fish from a pound up to 2 lb $2^1/_2$ oz. They fought well in the extra push of water, straining the $1^1/_2$ lb hook length to the limit. I also hooked into something really huge which I thought at first was a monster roach, but after a few initial heavy thumps the rod was almost wrenched from my grasp as it sped downstream at a rate of knots. Obviously a big old brownie which I doubt very much I could have brought upstream against such heavy water even if the hook had held.

Reluctantly, I left the swim with the roach going potty and drove back to Norwich and work.

Wednesday, 7 January

Overcast, mild, light SW wind.

Deciding to make hay while the sun shines, I have taken today and tomorrow off to stay with the mild weather and the big roach.

Doug Allen was at the house before dawn vowing that conditions were as good as they could possibly be. When we arrived at the river he was proved right, although the level had dropped a little and the colour was just about holding. Doug decided to walk upstream above the bend to fish the end of the long straight where he had taken a couple of roach to $1^3/_4$ lb before Christmas. I fished my usual "end" swim again and, on the second trot down, took a beautifully proportioned roach weighing 2 lbs 5 oz. It was a particularly deep fish (at present most are rather lean in the belly) short and with not a scale out of place.

This was a terrific start and yet, an hour later, apart from a brown trout of about a pound not another roach had shown on the surface or sucked in my maggots. This was rather puzzling because everything was so right for them to feed and, on the assumption that the shoal might have moved further down the swim, I allowed the float to trot another ten yards past its usual limit. It dipped smartly and out of the water flew a small dace. I batted it in upstream alongside my own bank and was about to lift it into the air when a huge head appeared and I was suddenly playing a double-figure pike.

I thought of breaking off but decided that its presence had already put the roach down so I might as well have a bit of fun. For about fifteen minutes I did just that although I could not raise it more than a foot from the bottom. I thought that I might eventually have a chance of beating it but was proved wrong.

In the meantime, Doug had wandered downstream to tell me he was getting bites and to see what all the fuss was about. After a chat I decided to try upstream of him where some good roach were priming on the surface. We stopped at his swim on the way upstream for elevenses and then I moved fifty yards above him to a spot between two bushes. This was a nicely positioned swim but a very short trot with limited vision due to the bush on my left. I put in a few maggots and swam through a few times to get the depth. After about ten minutes I was into a good roach — about $1^3/_4$ lb. And so was the next, and the next, and so on until after the ninth fish they went off. All were between 1 lb 10 oz and 1 lb 14 oz, all males wearing knobbly white pre-spawning tubicles in their nostrils. I have never experienced this segregation with roach so early on in the season before. With dace, yes, when the males go all leathery and feel like sandpaper to the touch. But with roach, and all males together in a shoal, never before.

Doug meanwhile was enjoying himself hooking some good roach and I heard his yell, "This one's the two pounder, John". I took the camera and scales down to his swim in time to see him put the net under his long awaited catch. At 2 lb $3^1/_2$ oz, that roach gave Doug immense pleasure.

As there appeared to be plenty of fish in this upstream reach I decided to wander further upstream to the very top swim which I had never fished. The depth was a little better than elsewhere and, after adjusting the float, I had a nice thirty yard trot down fairly close to my own bank where dense beds of rotting brown rushes matted the margins.

It was now about two o'clock and I figured (rightly, thank heavens) that I could do a lot worse than stay here until dark. I fixed up a short, quiver tip, rod with a link ledger, just in case fish were moving as the light went, and catapulted some maggots into the head of the glide. After fifteen casts and about a dozen loads of free bait the float sank positively at the very tail of the swim. These were better quality fish and, in complete contrast to the previous swim, all females, smooth and round-headed. The first fish was just 2 lb, followed by another four at a few ounces lighter; then another of 2 lb 1 oz.

With almost every bite the shoal seemed to be moving upstream towards me, making the prospects of hitting a really big one excellent. Then I did just that — a really powerful fish which stayed on the bottom in midstream shaking its head for a few seconds before rushing off downstream. It took me several minutes to pump him upstream and then, just as I was feeling in control, a large clump of floating weed lodged itself over the float. My biggest roach all but beaten and I couldn't lift the float out of the water to pull the fish (which was running erratically around on a free line) towards the net! I wound float and fish well upstream and put the net below the surface, hoping that if I released the tension on the fish it would turn downstream into the net.

Five roach over 2 lbs (best 2 lb 13 oz).

Luckily it did — all 2 lb 13 oz of it. I could have kissed it but didn't have the time. I popped it in with the others and put the bait straight out into the swim again. Just two casts later I was into yet another big one. This was a powerful as the previous fish but, managing to avoid floating weed, I had it safely in the net inside two minutes and then on to the scales which read a shaky (couldn't keep my hands still) 2 lb 10 oz.

I put the thirteen-footer down because the light was fading fast and flicked out the link ledger rod, with three maggots on a size 12 hook. Instantly, the flimsy quivertip twanged and another roach of about $1^3/_4$ lb made its way into the net. It looked almost small compared to those two previous fish. One can lose perspective all too easily when big fish come readily and in numbers. I almost wished it were possible to take one's big fish only every now and then instead of all at once.

With mixed feelings (I wanted to fish on into darkness but was physically and mentally exhausted) we packed the gear and headed for the car hoping that tomorrow would find the roach as eager to feed as today.

Thursday, 8 January

Overcast, moderate-to-fresh SW winds.

Doug came round even earlier this morning, in fact, we were so early that we sat in the car waiting for dawn to break.

We both made for the swims where we ended yesterday and I wished him good luck as I made for the big roach glide. Unfortunately, the wind had freshened overnight making presentation only just possible, but the roach (bless them) were still there and feeding, at least in my swim, and within five minutes I was into a good fish of 2 lb 3 oz.

I lost the next two fish. Both were very large indeed and came unstuck after about thirty seconds. The hook looked good but, to be safe, I changed it to a size 12 from 14, and managed to net the next fish — a shade under 2 lb. The next cast produced a lovely little perch of around 8 oz and the next a roach of $1^3/_4$ lb. After taking five more roach between $1^1/_2$ lb and $1^3/_4$ lb, all went dead as the sun came up. I trotted on for another half hour and then noticed that the water close by the bank was really quite clear. In fact, too clear. The colour of yesterday had gone and so, I feared, was the chance of taking any more fish till later in the evening.

I walked down to see Doug whose bites had gone with the sun also. He trotted on for the rest of the day but both without so much as another touch. We half expected a short feeding spell to materialize but, for some reason, this did not happen. As we left the sky was bright and as clear as the water; the moon shone down brightly and I rather imagine that those roach knew it and had finished their eating session.

AFTERTHOUGHT

If we have little or no rain by the weekend then conditions alone, particularly water clarity, will make big roach from the Wensum unlikely. We shall see. I shall probably go anyway. Perhaps I have made catching so many specimen roach look too easy. I have, in fact, been concentrating on these fish along this part of the Wensum for three years and the rewards of continually fishing for them have come at last.

Sunday, 11 January

Very overcast, strong westerly wind, very mild

As this mild winter weather is holding (55° at midday for the past five days) I decided to ring Andy Jubb yesterday evening in case he fancied another crack at the big roach on the Wensum and, of course, he did.

We arrived at first light to find a strong wind blowing across the river which was a shade higher than last Thursday with just a tinge of colour to it. Andy decided to fish the first swim as I wanted to again try the upstream glide which produced the 2 lb 13 oz fish.

We fixed up our tackle the previous evening and broke the rods down, an elastic band at each end keeping them together. By doing this we save those vital frenzied minutes of tackling up in the half light when, if feeding, big roach will be taking strongly. This morning our foresight really paid off. I found myself into fish on the third trot down — a roach of about $1^1/_2$ lb — and felt pleased that a shoal was still in residence in the swim. The main group was situated a long way downstream but, by feeding a dozen or so maggots every swim down, I soon had them biting at about ten yards range. For a good hour I expected a bite on every trot, and netted fourteen fish (pricked just one) from a pound upwards, with several at or around the $1^3/_4$ lb mark, to one of 2 lb 1 oz. Then bites ceased.

I took a stroll downstream to see how Andy was faring. He was not at all happy because, as he was about to net a good roach, a big pike came up and relieved him of it. At once I suspected the near-nineteen-pounder I had taken from the same spot in November because twice, since then, it has appeared on the scene to ruin sport. After losing the roach, Andy had taken a few dace and nothing else so I suggested he came upstream with me.

I tried a trot down when back at my swim to show Andy they had gone off and where bites had come from and, at that moment, the float disappeared. "I thought you said they'd gone off", said Andy, as I allowed a big fish to take line off the centre pin. It came in fairly easily after the initial run and, after a few thumps under the rod tip, I put the net under a 2 lb 7 oz roach. Nice one! However, try as I may — and I tried — there was no further

A 2lbs 7oz roach safely in the net

response. In fact, shortly after weighing the fish, strong sunlight scorched through the heavy cloud to such an extent that I regretted wearing my polar suit with a roll-neck jumper on top.

I suggested to Andy that the brightness meant we were unlikely to catch any more roach so why not try for the pike back at his swim before going home for lunch. The snag was that I only had my thirteen-foot trotting rod, but I doubted a pike would do it any harm. I exchanged my match aerial for a small fixed spool reel holding 7 lb line still in my tackle bag from last September's zander fishing trips and threaded on a small bung above a wire trace. On went a duo of size 8 trebles, we packed up the rest of my gear after returning the roach and trudged back to Andy's swim.

He had a few small dace on his net and one went on the trace and into the swim where the pike liked to lie. Almost immediately there was a huge "boil" two feet from the float which promptly shot away but the dace outran the pike. I reeled in and flipped it out again. The very same thing happened but this time the pike didn't miss. I tightened up and remembering that it was my trotting rod, struck firmly but lightly. Line sizzled from the reel in long powerful runs and, for the next five or six minutes, I experienced an unforgettable fight.

My arm was aching when Andy put the net under the very fish I had caught from that spot in November, but on this occasion it weighed a shade less at 18 lb 6 oz. I was quite tempted to remove her, but, after looking at her for a few seconds (deep and beautifully marked as only river pike are), I couldn't do it. Back she went — I hope I don't regret it in the future, though.

AFTERTHOUGHT

A great morning's sport. Felt thoroughly elated again especially with a good pike in addition to a couple of roach over 2 lb. Poor old Andy still hasn't cracked the water, but he will.

Tuesday, 13 January

Still very mild, overcast, light westerly wind.

My wife is becoming depressed about this mild weather and my ever-present urge to be long-trotting for roach. I may be pushing marital bliss to the limit but I just can't help myself and set out for the roach again this morning at first light. Although I had only an hour's actual fishing time I found the roach feeding. I fished the top glide and finished with seven fish, having pricked three. One of 2 lb 4 oz and the rest from $1^1/_4$ lb — all on either two or three maggots to a size 12 fine wire spade-end beneath a 3 AA peacock quill.

The river is becoming quite clear now and I doubt if the roach will feed on past the first hour, or until the last hour unless we have more rain. Because of this, I think I'll have another pike trip this Thursday and give the roach swims a rest. I should hate to overfish the stretch to the extent that only exceptionally light line to tiny hooks will bring bites. I always seem to lose fish when fishing overlight and I dread to think of that three-pounder coming adrift if I hook it.

Thursday, 15 January

Overnight ground frost, slight westerly wind, not too cold, variable cloud and sunny periods.

As the conditions were not particularly favourable for roaching, Doug Allen and I decided to have another crack at the pike in "the Conifers" lake. With our trip of New Year's day fresh in our minds when we missed so many runs, we were eager to fare better and made sure of a good supply of fresh herrings and live dace to use for live bait and wobbling. After making a late start, due to catching some livebaits on route, we rowed out to the same area as last time, about eighty yards from the shore at about nine-thirty.

In two hours of fishing two livebait rods with the rest on static float-fished herrings we accounted for two double-figure fish: a $16^1/_4$ lb fish to Doug and a 17 pounder to me — both accepting the static herring. But as no further runs materialized we moved after lunch to a position roughly in the middle of the lake with a depth of fifteen feet all around us. Within half an hour I took another double of around 11 lb, again on a static herring, and pulled out of another two. Each run came from the rod being fished upwind while the downwind baits remained untouched, though they were covering a wide area and were being twitched in a little every few minutes.

With about two hours of the day left I decided to concentrate on wobbling the dace as deadbaits due to the ineffectiveness on the paternoster tackle. I killed one and, after puncturing its swim bladder, put a swan shot on the trace twelve inches in front of it. The bait really worked a treat when wound in slowly but irregularly and I soon found an eight-pounder hanging on the other end. Then I took a three pounder, followed by another six all between 7 lb and 9 lb within a hectic forty-five minute spell. Missed another four takes.

Meanwhile, scoffing at my jacks, Doug was persevering with the static herrings and lost a fish of about 15 lb close to the boat, confirming our theory that the larger of these lake pike certainly prefer a static bait. But it was his only run of the afternoon. I guess I am just too impatient and, if I want to take a big one here, I shall just have to rest my backside — it is easier wobbling standing up.

In any event, we are certainly learning more about the lake and the areas most likely to produce fish. Today's tally of ten pike is the best yet. All the fish were plump and, as usual, fought strongly. We wonder how well a really big fish will fight, if and when we hook it.

Douglas Allen getting the better of a 16 ¾lbs pike

Saturday, 17 January

Quite cloudy, light drizzle, not too cold, no wind.

I thought I would pop down to the top glide on the Wensum this morning; firstly, to see the state of the river and, secondly, to have an hours trotting before work. But it was a mistake. The river was very clear, quite slow, and I had only one bite resulting in a roach of 1 lb 11 oz on double maggot. They are obviously in the same swim but need colour in the water to feed well.

Thursday, 22 January

Quite mild, cloudy with very strong NW winds.

Due to the river Wensum running very low, Doug Allen and I decided to visit "the Conifers" lake again. We packed trotting rods in case poor sport persuaded us to spend the last two hours of daylight on the Wensum.

On arrival at the lake at dawn we found the boat out of the water for its yearly repairs and a north-west facer blowing onto the boat house stagings, the only bank fishing spot (due to thick woods surrounding the margins) on the lake. This was bad news as our favourite spot lies some eighty yards from shore. Nevertheless, we punched out herrings, some on float tackle to drift back to us along the bottom, and others static-ledgered. The trouble was, the baits were blown straight back at us and we found that thirty yards was maximum range. Doug lost a big double-figure pike which dived under the stagings after snapping up a herring on the retrieve. After two hours of wobbling a small herring over the same small area I netted a ten-pounder.

By lunchtime we had had enough and decided to make for the Wensum where, although conditions were not good, we did stand a chance with the roach, particularly as the day was so mild and despite the clearness of the water.

As it happened, we should have settled for the Wensum in the first place because, almost from the start, we contacted roach — and some nice ones at that. Doug took nine to 2 lb 3 oz and myself twenty-four to 2 lb 1 oz. All took double maggot on size 14 hooks and came readily at the end as the light faded and the wind dropped. Strangely enough, amongst my catch were a dozen fish under the pound. I had not expected that many young roach here. Doug would have taken more fish if a big pike had not seized a $1^{1}/_{2}$ lb roach and led him a dance for fifteen minutes before finally snipping through the hook length.

I have marked the spot just downstream from the bushes swim which is only fifty yards away from the glide where I have been taking all the roach. For the sake of our future roaching we shall have to do a removal job on the pike. He looked all of 15 lb.

Thursday, 29 January

Conditions Foul!, bitterly cold, strong SE wind — Bright sunshine which could not raise the temperature above zero all day.

Despite the conditions, Doug Allen and I decided to have a scratch-about day on Suffolk's river Waveney, near Bungay, simply because every single broad and lake in Norfolk is frozen solid. On our arrival at nine o'clock, the Waveney was fairly high, running fast and coloured with icy snow water. There was also a liberal coating of snow left in the meadows from last week's fall. Not really roaching conditions.

Nevertheless, my trotted single maggot on an 18 was sipped in second cast, half way along a favourite bend. A big roach belted off downstream and thumped for a while before kiting upstream; and then the hook popped out. An hour later I took a roach of about 14 oz and on the very next cast managed to foul-hook a ten-inch bream in the dorsal fin. Doug fished a long glide upstream from me and had only a few tiny bites which he missed. We stuck it until three o'clock and then could not get back to the car fast enough.

Sunday, 1 February

A bitingly cold east wind, cloudy, temperature zero.

The temperature has not risen above freezing for five days. I drove to the Wensum, wobbled a herring close to the bottom between the ice floes for half-an-hour, and gave up.

I then drove to the river Tud, a feeder of the Wensum. The main flow was completely frozen over but a small overshoot weir pool was free, though green and icy looking. I put in a few maggots near the tail end of the flush and stret-pegged two on a 14 over them. The rest I fed to a little robin which appeared from nowhere when I took the lid off my maggot tin. An hour's fishing was enough and a small brown trout followed by a 3 oz dace were reward enough. I realised that all I really wanted to do, even in these appalling conditions, was to wet a line. With that done, I set off merrily for lunch.

I met John Judge today, who told me of a 9 lb bream he caught last week from the Wensum on flake fished after dark whilst after big roach. The river certainly is full of surprises and his bream must rate as one of the best ever to come from the Wensum. He caught it from a run I had fished last summer on four occasions each without a bite.

Thursday, 5 February

Conditions still very cold, just above freezing, a bitterly cold east wind.

Most still waters are still frozen, so this morning after breakfast I popped over to the river Waveney at Earsham for some scratchy roach fishing. My main interest was to field-test in bad conditions a revolutionary new match rod made from carbon fibre. The rod is on loan from a southern match fishing friend who asked me to try it out long-trotting for roach. At $14^1/_2$ feet, with butt and tip diameters of just thirteen-sixteenth and one sixteenth inches and weighing only 7 oz, it sliced easily through the strong wind.

This super rod performed really well. I hit the few bites I had easily without excessive arm movement and, when hooked, a roach was a joy to play. The virtue of carbon, apart from its lightness, is the steeliness one feels whilst casting, striking and playing — most reminiscent of a good quality built-cane rod. There is none of the spongey feeling of hollow glass. One feels in direct contact at all times and, of course, it is so light that long trotting for hours on end is an absolute joy.

But the roach were very finicky due to the clear, cold water and the east wind. I packed up after taking a dozen or so fish up to a pound.

Sunday, 8 February

Cold southerly wind — overnight frost.

Went along to the Wensum to try some trotting but the wind and very clear water were against it. Fished from dawn for two hours. Nothing.

Friday, 13 February

Hint of rain behind the clouds and a strong northerly wind.

This morning's weather conditions gave me just a faint chance of some roach sport, so, at daybreak, I popped down to my favourite stretch of the Wensum for a two-hour pre-work session. The river was still fairly clear and surprisingly, quite low despite some heavy rain during the past few days.

I fished the "top" upstream glide which has been my best hope of a monster roach just lately and, despite today being both the 13th and a Friday, I was in luck.

The one and only bite of the session, to double maggots on a size 14 long trotted close to the bottom, resulted in a beautifully proportioned and conditioned roach of exactly 2 lb 12 oz. My second best to date.

Sunday, 15 February

Quite cold and frosty, not much wind.

I visited the Wensum close to home again this morning but it was very clear, low and non-productive.

In the evening I fished with John Judge and John Bailey on their stretch of the Wensum near Lyng.

However, after two very cold hours fishing from 4.30 to 6.30 p.m. without so much as a twitch we packed up.

Tuesday, 17 February

Very overcast with low-lying clouds, light but cold easterly wind.

Both Doug Allen and I were looking forward to today because we had finally managed to obtain permission to pike fish a private broad. It is a large water, with rushes and alders along the margins, which are nowhere more than four feet deep. We call it "the Flats". The winter winds colour the shallow water quite thickly and so it lends itself wonderfully to presenting the dead herring, either fished static or drifted along on the float.

At eight-thirty a.m. we rowed out from the boathouse and positioned the boat in the lee of a peninsular, out of the east wind, where we could present static herrings over an area which had produced several 20 lb plus pike for Doug last winter. Sheltered as we were, our baits were still dragged along by surface movement but, by fishing well over depth, they held quite well almost where-ever we put them. At about ten o'clock I saw one of my celluloid floats swimming against the ripple and we quickly reeled in the other baits to give me a wide playing area. We were expecting to contact one of the heavy females which lurk in the broad, and so it turned out. The very second I set the hooks a long pike boiled on the surface showing us its huge tail. It then made a series of heavy, short runs and came in quite easily until it saw the boat. Doug had warned me of this from his past experiences here and I slackened the clutch to let it have its last run. Doug made a good job of the netting and there at the bottom of the boat lay my first twenty-pounder — 22 lb 12 oz to be exact. After taking nearly one hundred doubles, with several near misses, I had finally made it.

Thirty minutes later I had another run and, after a spirited fight, Doug put the net under a fifteen pounder. Then it was his turn for some action. As his float slid positively away he said that this was another twenty (big females seem to take so positively and slowly) and by the way it fought I could not disagree. This fish fought far harder than mine and for several minutes made a series of fast, powerful runs. It veered round to his right and went behind the boat where I put the net under it for him. It was another twenty at 20 lb 12 oz.

This sort of sport is almost unbelievable until it happens and, after returning the fish, we were really keyed up for action. But from 11 o'clock till three o'clock our floats lay motionless. We decided to move our position forward some eighty yards to cover the end of the bay for the last two hours fishing, and rowed slowly to the spot from which the runs had come. Short casting close to the boat produced nothing so I whipped a herring out a good sixty yards to my left in very shallow water close to the bank. A few minutes later the float shook and, after turning round, came moving slowly towards me. I had no choice but to hit it immediately but still the fish swam towards me. It felt very large, indeed, and veered off under the other lines to my right where it surfaced close to the boat. I held it fairly tightly while Doug lifted the lines from the water and, after a couple of heavy swirls, I drew it over the huge landing net.

One twenty in a day's fishing would have suited me fine but this fish had made a good day into a truly memorable one. She was a very deep-bodied

C

The author with one of his twenties

fish, better than the first, and sent the spring balance down to 23 lb 12 oz. Apart from having one blind eye she was in magnificent shape and I lovingly slipped her back after the photography session.

It was now nearly five and darkness began to loom over the broad. We reluctantly pulled up the weights and, while I rowed back bubbling about the day's catch, Doug put the tackles down. What a day's piking! Just four runs in nine hours but four fish for $82\frac{1}{2}$ pounds.

A red letter day, indeed.

Thursday, 19 February

Misty, overcast hint of frost but pleasant.

After Tuesday's excitement, Doug and I visited "the Conifers" Lake today for some down-to-earth piking. The boat was back in the water again and, as dawn broke and shrouded in thick mist, we rowed out to our usual place hoping, as usual, for a big one to turn up but expecting the usual catch of a

Douglas Allen with a brace of big roach

couple of doubles plus a few jacks; and that is exactly what we caught. Doug had pike of 15 lb, 11 lbs and 4 lbs to my two of 12 lb and 7 lb. All accepted the static herrings, as did several small jacks which came adrift.

Curiously, when we rowed out at first light the lake was clear of ice. Yet by about half past nine the surface had frozen and for an hour and a half we sat there helpless not able to get a bait any more than a few feet down before the line stuck on the ice.

Saturday, 21 February

Very misty, damp and mild, river very clear.

Doug Allen and I decided to roach the Wensum this morning for two hours before work. Despite the river being clear the light values were low due to the mist, and we were optimistic.

Doug fished the 'bush' swim below the long glide I have been fishing lately and took five roach — the best two weighing 2 lb and 2 lb 5 oz, his best to date. He would have taken more but the pike which took a roach from Doug's hook on his last trip appeared for a repeat performance. I couldn't raise a bite in the long glide and so I took Doug's smallest roach (about 8 oz) and decided to have a bash at his troublesome pike. Within minutes the pike grabbed the bait but very quickly came unstuck. I again put the roach out, and again the pike grabbed it and ejected on the strike. By then it was time for us to head for work, but we shall certainly catch that pike in the near future.

Sunday, 22 February

River very clear, light southerly wind, mild.

After getting to bed late following a lengthy dinner party, I went along to the Wensum for an afternoon session.

The sky was quite clear and I suspected that bites would not materialise until the light began to fade. Unfortunately the roach did not show until I had only about a dozen casts left before I could see no longer. Result, three roach to just over the pound.

A rather disappointing session and, unless we have some substantial rain soon, sport won't improve.

Tuesday, 24 February

Light west wind — very mild.

I fancied an hour's fishing on the way home from work this evening and went along to the tiny river Tud at Ringland for some long-trotting.

From half past five to six o'clock, when I could no longer see the float I took three dace to 10 oz and two roach of about a pound apiece, all on maggots. I would have loved to have stayed but, as Barbara had my dinner waiting and as I am off work all day tomorrow for a piking trip, I don't want to push her too far.

Wednesday, 25 February

Moderate westerly wind, very mild.

I picked up Doug Allen at six-fifteen this morning and we set off for yet another extensive broad where Doug had obtained permission for a day's piking.

We had a good supply of fresh herrings which we hoped might account for some sizeable pike. These particular pike do not live in the broad, but migrate each year at about this time from the nearby river Bure. They gather at the western end of the broad in just two feet of water, surrounded by marshland and drainage dykes, as an early grouping process prior to spawning. The broad, itself, is quite large — about fifty acres. At the western end, via a narrow inlet, there is a bayou of about four acres. It is secluded, private, and very pikey.

We put the mud weights down alongside a small island giving us a wide area over which to drift our baits downwind towards the bayou's inlet. Within minutes the pike, which must have been scouring the bottom (there is little or no food in the broad in the winter), found our herrings and we had at least twelve runs in a hectic sixty-minute spell. I was treated to eight of them, resulting in seven pike to 16 lb. All but the largest — a fresh, nicely-marked fish which could not have left the river very long ago — were jacks between four and seven pounds. One little fellow of around 4 lb actually came to my rod twice. The first time he took a whole herring and the second time, about two hours later, he picked up a half bait. I knew it was the same fish, for it had a nasty gaff wound under its chin and a blood spot in the roof of its mouth

37

where my hooks went in on the first encounter. A strange occurrence this, as I never retain small fish in the keep net. Were it not for the nasty gaff wound, I doubt if I would have known. Why on earth anglers still use gaffs on pike, especially little ones easily picked out of the water by hand, I shall never know. Unfortunately, each of Doug's four runs resulted in pricked fish — one a very large pike. It was not his day.

This hectic feeding spell ended at nine and we waited expectantly for the rest of the day till darkness without another run.

Thursday, 26 February

Moderate westerly wind, very mild, 58° at midday.

I had not intended to get out of various household chores today, such as digging the garden, etc., but I could not resist a short evening trip. I fished the upper Bure near Oxnead from four-thirty p.m. till well on into darkness and missed the only bite of the evening on breadflake — possibly a roach.

Chris Gooch with his opening-day pike of 25lbs

Sunday, 28 February

Very overcast, moderate SW wind, brighter later.

I was looking forward to my annual pilgrimage to Ranworth Inner Broad today. For the past four years on opening day (the broad is only open for the last two weeks of the coarse season once the shooting season has finished) at least two 20 lb — plus pike have been boated.

However, and despite conditions being tantamount to perfection for piking, just two pike were the reward shared between some eighteen anglers who took boats out to fish. As usual I blanked but my friend, Chris Gooch a fellow Broadlands Specimen Group member, took one of the pike — a beauty of 25 lb 6 oz on a static herring, a new group record. We recognised the fish as being the very same taken by Reg Sandys on the last opening day when it weighed $28^1/_2$ lb. Bill Giles caught it the year before at $28^1/_4$ lb. What a friendly pike.

I left the broad at midday and, having already obtained some small livebait which I left in the car fed by a battery oxygen pump, made my way to a lake in North Norfolk, near Cromer, in search of some perch. I had feared Ranworth would not produce many fish and felt pleased that I had planned an alternative afternoon's sport; but I blanked again at the lake. I did hook two fish, though, both on gudgeon baits. One was well in excess of 2 lb. In all I must have had a dozen or so runs but they were very timid and I found it impossible to set the hook properly.

I enjoyed today's fishing — despite not landing a single fish — and really must concentrate my efforts on some perch in the future.

Wednesday, 3 March

Freezing cold east wind after overnight frost, bright sunshine.

Today was to be full of promise and big pike, for Doug and I had obtained permission to fish the 'Flats' again where we caught the three twenty-pounders a fortnight ago. But the weather conditions were all wrong. To start with, the shallow water was pathetically clear and, with a strong easterly wind to chill it plus bright sunshine from dawn till dusk, our chances of taking a big fish were very slim. We covered the same area which produced the big fish

39

last time out and boated fish of 6 lb, 9 lb and 13 lb, with one run missed.

All were females and accepted our standard static herring bait during the first two hour's fishing. We moved position several times during the remainder of the session, all to no avail, and by five p.m. we were so cold that the thought of sitting in the car with the heater full on held more promise than waiting it out till dark in the vain hope of a last-minute run.

Thursday, 4 March

Light easterly wind after overnight frost, warm, bright sunshine.

After yesterday's freezing easterly wind, I didn't really relish another day's herring bashing. But Doug and I had already booked "the Conifers" lake (luckily, for the morning only) so naturally I was up with tackle at the ready when he pushed the door bell at half past six.

We both felt very tired indeed but, within minutes of mooring the boat over our favourite patch in twelve feet of water, one of Doug's floats started moving off across the surface and the adrenalin quickly dispelled the yawns. Doug soon had a plump female of around 13 lb inside the boat and then one of my floats shot off — another double of 11 lb. No sooner had we unhooked and returned her than Doug was in again and into a better fish. It was another female of around 15 lb which regurgitated three partly-digested herrings and the head of a sprat in addition to Doug's herring. Someone had obviously fished the same location quite recently and thrown their bait remains in. They had, in all probability, caught this same fish too because one of its jaws was badly mutilated and the hook had actually fallen out in the landing net.

The next three runs amounted to a jack of about 5 lb for me, a missed run for Doug and then a lost fish for me. Unlike every other pike in this deep lake, which bore deep and stay deep until they are ready for netting, this one peeled off quite a few yards of line coming straight to the surface some sixty yards out. I pumped it along the top for a spell but, when it dived, the hooks pulled out. I was quite sick, being certain that it would have made well over double figures — if not more. We fished on from ten o'clock till one, during which time the sun had obviously put the pike off the prowl.

An interesting morning — I am looking forward to my next and last trip of the season to the lake next Wednesday. My brother Dave is staying with us

A nice one for Douglas

for a few days next week and I have promised him some double-figure pike and 2 lb roach. The pike, yes, but roach without rain — doubtful.

Sunday, 7 March

Very cold, fresh easterly wind, light snow showers, bright sunshine.

I overslept this morning, though with the present weather conditions I might as well have stayed in bed.

Nevertheless, I set off for the perch lake where I missed several runs last Sunday armed with a good supply of small dace. For an hour I fished them below floats without a touch and then switched over to ledgering. I missed the first bite (very gentle) but hit the next, a lovely-looking, deep bellied perch of around the pound. The following, and last, bite resulted in the tiniest pike I think I have ever caught — seven inches long.

The session only lasted for an hour and a half because I felt so cold, but I intend visiting the lake again tomorrow for another try, weather permitting. I have four days off work this week which I had intended to use in pursuit of big roach but the Wensum under these appalling weather conditions is completely off the cards. The very same thing happened last year when I took the last week off.

Monday, 8 March

Very cold, light NE wind, light snow showers, bright sunshine.

This morning, (after setting out at nine) was almost a repeat performance of yesterday. I visited the perch lake armed with some worms and small livebaits and fished two rods until one p.m. without so much as a nibble. Perhaps the fresh easterly wind of yesterday had chilled the water too much.

After leaving the lake I made tracks for the upper Yare near Bawburgh, just five miles west of Norwich and only four miles from home. I fancied that moving water would offer the best prospects in this cold weather and I carted the small livebaits (two-inch dace) along the river to an eight-foot hole on the downstream corner of a double S bend where I knew perch and chub to be. I had, in fact, taken a 5 lb $2^1/_2$ oz chub from this swim last winter whilst roach fishing. It is the sort of little river where almost anything can take hold.

In the space of two hours, from three until five, I had a dozen runs on my little baits. Those I connected with materialized into seven pike and one perch of $1^1/_4$ lb. The pike were tiny, between 6 oz and $1^1/_2$ lb and barely took the float under. Two of the missed runs could possibly have been chub for they were very fast 'positive' takes. The others were sizeable perch which unfortunately came adrift.

Wednesday, 10 March

Fresh southerly winds, quite cold.

I visited "the Conifers" lake again today in the company of Doug Allen. Armed with a good supply of fresh herrings we roamed over the entire lake from dawn till dusk, giving each area an hour with the static herrings and occasionally drifting one along with the wind.

Even our favourite spot failed to produce a run. The only excitement came when a pike of about 10 lb surfaced close to the boat, took a brief look at us, and then dived down again. A few minutes later one of Doug's floats twitched and bobbed but did nothing else. On the retrieve there were no teeth marks and we assumed that the inquisitive pike must have bumped into the line. The water was very coloured with a visibility of only a few inches. A most inexplicably disappointing blank day.

It was perhaps good fortune for my brother Dave who was to have stayed with me today for a piking session at the lake, but who at the last minute could not make the trip from London. He is bound to laugh at my so-called guaranteed pike trips — when I ring him later.

Thursday, 11 March

Fresh southerly wind, very cold.

After yesterday's blank at a usually productive water Doug and I were not at all optimistic about today's venue, even though it was the same broad where we caught the three twenty-pounders a few weeks ago.

The southerly wind had a nasty stinging bite to it and when we arrived at the boat house at first light the water on the broad was so low (it is fed by the tidal river Bure) that the boat dyke had been reduced to a mud flat.

Luckily, one of the boats had been tied up at the entrance to the broad and this I managed to reach after wading through 200 yards of foul-smelling marshland. I then had to row it the whole length of the broad where a hard patch of land close to the road allowed Doug with the gear to get on board. Eventually, and after a dawn arrival at the water, we were fishing by nine o'clock. The only area which afforded us a depth in excess of two feet was the same area from where the big fish came, so we settled down upwind of the patch, lobbed out our herrings, and waited.

At ten-thirty, Doug had a run quite close to the boat and duly boated a long lean fish of $14^1/_2$ lb. Our optimism grew but we had to wait until half past four for the next run when I hit into a little jack of about four pounds. Then Doug had a fish slip the hook (almost certainly another jack) and I fared the same with my next and our last run of the day. I had too much line out after a long cast, aided by a tail wind which took the herring at least eighty yards across the broad. It was impossible to set the hooks at that distance. To add even more misery to a particularly cold day we found the level had dropped by six inches on our return to dry land and spent at least an hour pushing and shoving on the quant to make the last two hundred yards through liquid mud to where we had left the car. What a day!

Sunday, 14 March

Light easterly wind, cloudy, neither cold nor mild.

There was a time when I considered the 14th March the saddest day of the year. But nowadays I actually look forward to its arrival (which will allow me to catch up on the garden chores) and so, rather than try to end the season by going out with a bang, I merely want to catch some fish. Any fish.

Andy Jubb and I started today by visiting the Waveney at Earsham where, from first light until around nine o'clock, we (or rather Andy) took six roach to 14 oz. I blamed my stool coming apart for not catching much but, to be fair to Andy, I just could not interest anything in my swim after dropping a roach of around 12 oz. The river was pathetically low and clear.

We moved from the river to a little farm pond in Bungay where I knew we could catch some small roach livebaits with a view to a spot of perch fishing afterwards. We amassed thirty little baits in just over an hour's fishing and set off for a gravel pit at Homersfield, five miles down the road, where perch are really easy to catch. We were not taking any chances on the 14th March.

The pit, though quite large at around 15 acres, was fairly crowded and we had a fair walk over to the other side to find some vacant swims. All the water is deep here, between 10 and 25 feet with small islands on top of the gravel bars where they shelve up from the deeps. Andy failed this time and could not tempt a perch whereas, just twenty yards away, I could not stop catching them. All were between 6 oz and 14 oz and gobbled the little livebaits down as soon as the bomb hit bottom.

After lunch we left the pit and drove back towards Norwich to where the river Yare flows beneath the A 146 Trowse road bridge. We fancied ending the day roach fishing the tidal pool at Trowse and so rented a boat from the cottage downriver at Whitlingham lane. Once anchored in the pool, with a nice streamy run of around six feet deep going away from the boat, we soon latched onto some roach around the pound mark. They accepted double maggot to 16 hooks and really thumped the rod in the strong current. But try as we might, we could not catch them from any particular spot. Andy had six and myself eight when we finally pulled the weights up at six o'clock.

We enjoyed the row back (well I did with Andy at the oars) talking of the season's sport; what we had caught and lost, where we were concentrating next season and the targets we still have. It was a lovely end to a particularly productive season but still nice to pack the rods up for a break. I hope the close season is never abolished, as some would have it, for I think we would be the losers.

Well, my wife would be, anyway.

THE CLOSE SEASON

THE CLOSE SEASON

There was a time when every spare hour of the close season would find me fish-spotting in my favourite haunts. Nowadays, due to the pressure of work in my tackle shop, I content myself with a few, spur of the moment, fly fishing outings along the upper Wensum or Tud, combined with as many scuba jaunts as close season decorating will allow.

I would dearly love to do more diving in the places I fish because looking at a fish's underwater world from his own view point can teach the angler a great deal.

One learns to appreciate just how inquisitive fish are and where certain species prefer to live — especially the larger specimens. One can watch their reactions to a baited hook and, looking at a line of three pounds breaking strain from two feet away, realise that there is no such thing as an invisible line. But, with their sight and radar system, they are always conscious of the angler's line, no matter how fine or camouflaged it may be. They still take the bait because much of their natural food is gathered by sucking in mouthfuls of weed which contains shrimps, caddis, snails, etc., after which they blow out the unwanted particles. To a fish, the line would appear as an unwanted object to be blown out once it has separated the bait from it.

Of course, if the angler is using a heavy nylon line which is not pliable, as all forms of weed are, the fish becomes suspicious. That is why finer lines (in the right circumstances) catch more fish; not because they are less visible, but because they are more supple and, as the fish moves away with the bait, they create less resistance.

I have observed many such things beneath the surface and, over the past few months, I have been promising myself a diving trip to sort out a problem I have been working on for quite some time. It is this: why do we miss so many bites (usually at distance) when ledgering?

I have thought about this problem quite deeply over the past two years and have been longing to stage a mock-up ledgering session with myself under the water with the fish, moving the ledger weight and bait as a fish would do, while friends on the bank try striking the bites I give them.

49

D

A Specimen Fishing Year

Last Sunday finally saw the experiment take place. The day was bright and sunny, the water not too cold (even in a thick wet suit it can be cold down below at this time of year) and the lake at Lenwade, near Norwich, where I had decided to stage the session was incredibly clear. John Bailey and John Judge were already at the lake, fish spotting, when I arrived accompanied by Sid Johnson and fellow members of the Broadland Specimen Group, who were keen to see what came out of the exercise. Steve Harper and Chris Gooch, who, like myself, do a lot of distance fishing for tench and bream, were particularly interested in the paternoster versus running lead and link ledger contest. You would, perhaps, naturally assume that a running ledger is more sensitive and I myself have been under this impression for a number of years, but the diving session taught me otherwise.

Once the rods (one with a link ledger, the other with a fixed paternoster, and both with two-foot hook trails) had been cast out some thirty yards from the bank, I swam out to see how they were lying on the bottom. Steve and Chris had pulled back after casting so that a straight line existed between hook and rod tip and the first bite I gave them was directly away from the rod. Both ledgers acted as I imagined they would and the pull I felt from the rods (I was holding a piece of plastic instead of a hook) was easily enough to set the hook, had there been one.

Then I swam at a right angle to the ledgers. I picked up the plastic disc of the link ledger and moved it two feet. At the rod, Steve had an eighteen-inch drop on his bobbin indicator and, as it rose to just under the rod, he struck. What I felt on the end was quite astounding. Initially, I felt only a slow "draw" followed by a heaviness as the link ledger bumped along the bottom to align itself between the rod and my hand. Only then did I feel the full impact of his strike.

This was most interesting and explained why so many of our bites at distance are missed or result in feeling the fish only momentarily. They obviously sense a slow build up in pressure and are literally drawn through the water till they eject the bait or at best find themselves hooked lightly in the lips.

We repeated the exercise over and over again and each time it was the same: the angle created between bait, ledger and rod when a fish swims off at right angles to the ledger (probably half of all bites) is just too great for the rod to straighten out, except on medium-to-short casts. We then ran through the same experiment on the paternoster tackle. When I moved the plastic disc at right angles to the ledger to create a bite the reel line and the paternoster link line both moved over in alignment with me. Here, I think, lies the secret of the paternoster's simplicity and effectiveness (though perhaps those anglers

50

already using the paternoster are not actually aware of this fact) because I felt the power of the strike *instantly* and the drag of the bomb afterwards. Remember, it was the reverse with the link ledger and would have been with any other type of running ledger weight regardless of how long the link, because if the lead stays put as the line passes through it the angle is made more acute.

Of course, the further you allow a fish to travel with the bait (if it moves off at right angles) the greater is the yardage of line to be picked up. With those tearaway bites which move directly away from you, one cannot, if using the paternoster, allow too long a run before striking lest the fish starts towing the lead. These types of bites — the kind one gets when carping — would be the only ones where I would not now use the paternoster. One thing to remember when paternostering is not to use too light a lead, in case it moves instead of the bobbin indicater. Remember that all objects, even lead, have a lower specific gravity in water. I would not use anything lighter than half an ounce, in conjunction with a light plastic bobbin or silver paper indicator.

I discovered the answer to another puzzle when I moved the plastic disc towards the rod to simulate a drop bite. For this experiment I had my head out of the water looking at both the bobbin on the rod and the ledger set up beneath the water. Just before the lead moved (this happened with both the running and the paternoster set-ups) and the silver indicator dropped back, the latter moved up a couple of inches. This was due to the U in the line tightening, not because a fish has moved away and then back towards the rod as I had always previously imagined.

It certainly seems to show that if you are getting a lot of drop bites preceded by short lifts of the indicator, you should strike before the indicator falls and the fish feels the lead, giving you surplus line to mend.

I found also, that even three swan shot on a link would be pulled back towards the rod instead of the line running through the split ring, and this on a hard gravel bottom. Of course, even if the line did pass through as the fish swims towards the angler, subsequent hooking of fish at distance is even worse than when trying to hit those right angle bites.

One particularly intriguing thing happened when I moved the disc back towards one of the rods which had a gravel bar between it and the lead. The line seemed to be held between the stones and I swam almost to the rod with the lead and hook line without the indicator moving either up or down. Can you remember one of those all-night (biteless) carping sessions when, on reeling in in the morning, you found your line in a huge vee and the terminal gear much closer in than you had cast it? This, of course, can happen even

51

The underwater experiment

more easily when freelining if the line cannot pass over large obstacles and is supported by them.

Many anglers have been using the simple paternoster all their angling lives and match anglers, in particular, are past masters with it. It does lend itself wonderfully hitting those fenland bream bites on the drop when using a long hook trail, and also when the bait has finally settled. But I wonder how many anglers there are, like me, who have never questioned the validity of the running ledger before. Indeed, nearly all those I have questioned who use the paternoster merely say that it works better than a running lead — but know not why. Well, perhaps my little underwater sortie helped put a few more pieces in the ledgering jigsaw puzzle.

Wednesday, 7 June

Humid weather — temperature at 80 plus for the past three days.

As I have not been doing much fishing or fish spotting for the past few weeks due to the pressure of work, tonight I finally decided to visit the tiny river

Tud, near Ringland, for a spot of trouting.

I arrived about eight o'clock and, after parking by the weir pool, walked slowly upstream to see what was about. Almost immediately a nice brownie scattered a fry shoal a little upstream of the weir. But I left him (I could not be bothered to catch some minnows) and found a dozen or so fish sucking in nymph cases some hundred yards upriver. Unfortunately they were clustered along the opposite bank and, as mine was too well planted with young willow trees for long casting, I decided to walk round to the other side. By now there was only a half hour of light left and I feverishly plopped a small fly onto the surface along the margins where the trout (taking little notice of me) were sipping in their supper.

For several minutes they ignored my offering (must remember to put some small nymphs in my box) and I feared that a take would never come. But then up popped a pair of lips — and I rolled it off. But only a few minutes later I made contact and was into a brownie of a pound plus — a goodish fish for this little river.

Unfortunately, though a few fish carried on swirling upstream, a brace was not to be and the feeding stopped before I lost sight of the fly. I walked upstream to try the others but they were not interested and so, complete with my supper for tomorrow, I motored home.

A very enjoyable evening.

AFTERTHOUGHT

It is a great pity that I always seem to find so little time during the close season for fly fishing. I find it very relaxing compared with my uptight specimen hunting sessions. But household chores such as repainting, gardening, etc., always seem to take precedence. And now, of course, with just nine days to go before the new season starts my attentions are concentrated on tench, rudd and bream.

I intend to concentrate on these three species this coming summer with perhaps a bit of chubbing thrown in when things are not going too well.

Friday, 11 June

Although I have been fish-spotting on countless occasions along the banks of the Wensum at my favourite "Rushes" stretch, and also searched for the roach shoals from a position in the bows of a boat, I had never dived this part of the river before. That is until this evening.

I had been looking forward to a 'dive' for some time due to this continual oppressively hot weather. The Wensum looked so beautifully 'clear' and the weed for this summer was still in its infancy when Sid Johnson and I decided to wander along the river bed to see if we could find the roach.

We plopped in at around seven o'clock armed with powerful diving torches in case we were overtaken by darkness (as we often are — time flies when underwater) but, after a few minutes down below, we realised that visibility was too poor to see much.

The river looked very clear from the bank when looking down through the water to the bottom, but once down below there was so much suspended phyto plankton through all water layers that visibility was limited to just two or three feet. We have often experienced this phenomenem when diving apparently clear waters, particularly gravel pits. It is most frustrating especially when you have lugged all the diving gear across a couple of fences and spent fifteen minutes getting geared up and the frustration is doubled when you finally realise that your fish-spotting efforts will be a waste of time.

Nevertheless, we did explore the river bed where dredging had taken place two years ago and in particular, the opposite bank from where I usually fish. I soon realised why my summer ledgering for roach is always more fruitful when the bait is placed close to the far bank. Instead of the river bed slowly shelving up to the margins there is a pronounced ledge left from the dredgers channel, though the centre channel where I usually trot during the winter was, as I had suspected, very even.

The only fish we saw clearly were eels (some goodish ones to around the $2^1/_2$ lb mark) and a few small jacks. There were a few roach about but, due to the poor visibility, only the occasional blurred glimpse of them was seen as the shoal shot off upstream ahead of us.

A disappointing evening as far as fish spotting was concerned but beautifully cool down below.

A NEW SEASON

A NEW SEASON

Wednesday, 16 June

Dark, windy evening to the 15th and throughout the night, with occasional spells of fine drizzle, cool.

After nearly three weeks of continual hot and sunny weather I had hoped that today of all days would have been likewise, but no. Just a few hours before midnight heavy clouds spread quickly over the whole of Norfolk. It was a bad omen for Terry Houseago and me, considering that we had spent the past three "Opening Nights" intent on catching tench but blanking three years on the trot, and getting a soaking for our troubles on each occasion.

We picked a lake in North Norfolk where last summer, during a long seven-week assault on specimen tench, three members of the Broadland Specimen Group and myself took over two hundred tench in excess of 4 lb with over fifty of them five-pounders.

The marsh lake, as we call it, is a long and fairly wide water about 400 by 150 yards. The banks are completely open and the water always gin clear. Depth varies from two feet at one end down to eight feet at the other. In the middle was an area about five feet deep which, last year, produced most of our fish though we did pick up a few in the deep water. There is little weed growth in the middle and just light blanket weed around the margins. Quite an easy water to fish, really, though hooking these particular tench at a distance of sixty yards does present some problems — but more of that later.

Terry and I arrived at the Marsh a little before dark and there met Steve Harper and Martin Page who were tackled up and all ready for the off. Steve had seen a few patches of bubbles in our favourite spot and had catapulted out some balls of ground bait laced with maggots. All our fish last season came to bunches of maggots on size 10 hooks to a swim feeder rig. Steve decided to fish on the other bank, directly opposite Terry, Martin and myself. As a whole year had passed since our last visit, we wondered whether our feeder rigs and maggots would be as effective so each decided to fish maggots on one rod and a different bait on the other.

With the new season just thirty minutes old a shout of "I'm in" from the opposite bank indicated that Steve was into a tench and, after a strong fight, he lifted out a big male of 4 lb 3 oz. It fell to a lobworm. Terry and I persevered with flake as alternate bait but by now, Martin could not resist fishing maggots on both rods. He had some bites, too, but just slight twitches. Then his bobbin shot up and he was fast into an eel which subsequently weighed in at 2 lb.

At half past one in the morning the rain became too damp so we all piled into the tent for a couple of hours sleep. Martin managed to summon up enough energy to return to his rods at daybreak and yelled out when bites started to materialize. Teeth chattering, we resumed the maggot and feeder bombardment and within minutes Martin was into a heavy fish, a plump female of 5 lb 13 oz. He was really pleased as it beat his previous best (caught here last year) by an ounce. I knew it was a good tench when he struck because he said he had hooked an eel. Whenever Martin makes a prediction about what is on the other end, he is always wrong. His next bite was a real thumper which he called out was a small male tench and which turned out to be a super perch of exactly $2^1/_2$ lb — another personal best. Then he did it again, but without the prediction, and had another tench of 5 lb 11 oz.

Although only a few yards separated Martin from Terry and me, we started to think about moving, because neither of us had had so much as a twitch. The fish certainly seemed to be directly in front of Martin. This was proved almost instantly by Steve who had lobbed a bait from the other side across to the far end of Martin's patch and was fast into a big tench. After a heavy, slow fight (so characteristic of big females) Steve lifted her onto the grass and quickly onto the scales: dead on 6 lb and his personal best. At least Steve and Martin had kicked off with a bang but as it was nearly seven o'clock — only an hour to go before heading for work — Terry and I were on the point of declaring our usual blank opening night. Then a strange thing happened: I actually had a good bite!

Immediately, and quite instinctively, I knew that this was a really big tench — slow but powerful, as it kited some twenty yards across Terry's lines. I followed it along the bank and was glad of Terry's eagerness to net it. It broke surface close in, made a short roll and then Terry had it in the net. What a beauty! Really deep set, short and dark gold. Martin hoisted it onto the Avons and gave the weight at a shade over 6 lb 3oz. I, too, had beaten my previous best.

I was over the moon and could have packed up for work there and then but Terry had yet to make a start. So we fished on till eight o'clock while Martin took two more tench of 5 lb 4 oz and 5 lb and then we just had to leave.

I felt sorry for Terry because it would really have made our morning had he taken one, but we all have days like this. We left Martin and Steve to fish on while I made for work, and Terry to take his kids to school.

We shall both be back again at the lake in the morning, and Sid Johnson is joining us.

What a really terrrific start to the season.

Martin Page, Steve Harper and the author with a memorable opening day catch.

Thursday, 17 June

Very little wind, misty and cool at dawn but sunny and very warm later.

Sid had to wake me this morning at 2.45 a.m. by banging on the front door as the alarm clock had failed. But the tiredness soon drifted away as we motored towards the marsh for some more tench. For Sid's benefit, I ran through the sort of tackle we use, mentioning that Martin and Steve would probably already be fishing and that swim feeders were the order of the day. I also told him that Martin had phoned last night to say that he had taken another big tench an hour after I had left yesterday. It weighed a massive 6 lb 6 oz and fell to our standard 4 maggots on a 10 hook. His and Steve's tally of fish for yesterday morning ended at twelve tench, nine over 5 lb, including two over 6 lb and the 2$^1/_2$ lb perch. What a catch!

On arrival at the lake we hurried across the field towards the lake and saw Steve's rod, bent in full curve, clearly visible through the thin mist. They were picking up the odd bite and this was the first fish of the session which he netted while I was frantically trying to unravel my ledger bobbins. It was a tench of 5 lb 12 oz.

Sid and I positioned ourselves on either side of the others and, within minutes, we started to get twitches but the tench in front of me were quite timid compared to Steve's swim. The bites were real tearaways in this hot spot. Within an hour or so Steve added another five fish to his tally — all, unbelievably, over the magical 5 lb mark. Then the main concentration of fish moved across in front of Martin and myself. Martin drew first blood and, in quick succession, netted two male fish of around 3 lb. My first was 5 lb 9 oz, followed by others of 5 lb 8 oz, 5 lb 3 oz and 4 lb 6 oz — all beautifully deep-bodied females. Then Martin took another one, in this same feeding spell, of 5 lb 2 oz before the cycle ended. All the bites were reasonable to strike at, even at sixty yards, and the bobbin lifting three to six inches. A mere quarter inch lift we call a twitch.

The time was now 7.30 a.m. and we saw Terry Houseago walking across the field towards the lake. Even after his all night shift in a furniture factory he could not resist the tench bonanza. He tackled up and moved in expectantly to my right. At this point, Sid, on the extreme left of the line, started to get bites and, after missing several and snapping off on two, finally put a nice female of 4 lb 12 oz on the bank — his biggest tench to date.

Uncannily, Terry remained fishless and, when I had to leave at eight o'clock for work, he was still staring down at his ledger bobbins.

A few hours after opening up the shop, Terry, Martin and Sid came in to tell me how they finished. Steve, who had all the initial action, never had another bite; whereas Sid took two more of 4 lb 1 oz and 3 lb 7 oz and Martin added another five pounder to his list — a fish of 5 lb 3 oz which was hooked through the dorsal fin and led him a dance for ten minutes. Terry again blanked, but I have a feeling that when he finally does sit in front of them when they are feeding he will shame us all.

AFTERTHOUGHT

Hopefully, and provided my eyes open when the alarm bell rings, I intend to have another crack tomorrow morning.

If the events of last season on the lake repeat themselves the next two or three sessions should be the best, both in number of bold bites and of fish caught. The best bag I had last season at this time was eleven fish in a morning for over 50 lb. After this catches dwindled as did the positive bites and after a few trips we were down to lots of tiny twitches which were so difficult to hit at range.

But we shall see.

Friday, 18 June

Very misty, chilly morning, slight breeze.

Again I managed to rise at 2.30 a.m. and, by the time I had motored to the 'marsh', dawn was breaking. Steve, Martin and Sid were already fishing and getting bites.

I sat next to Martin and was soon in the area with two baits out, though I had to wait a considerable time for a bite and my only fish of the session was a female of 4 lb 14 oz. Sid fared likewise and grassed a 4 lb 4 oz female, while Martin and Steve were again having a field day. They both took three tench apiece up to the $5^1/_2$ lb mark and were still getting bites when I left for work at eight. Later this afternoon Martin came into the shop to tell me the news: from nine to ten-thirty a.m. he accounted for a really superb tench brace during a mad feeding spell. One was 6 lb $^1/_2$ oz and the other a real lunker of 6 lb 10 oz. As always all the fish fell to maggots on the feeders.

These fish, combined with the massive overall weight of the others, have made us all realise that the magical seven-pounder might very well be just around the corner.

Sunday, 20 June

Very windy, overcast morning quite chilly until nine a.m. when the sun broke through.

Being a Sunday, this morning should have been a field day for me because I was able to fish on past my usual eight o'clock deadline when Martin and Steve have taken most of the bigger fish. Unfortunately, although I concentrated from dawn till eleven o'clock, I had but three bites of which I hit two, both spawned out females of 4 lb 9 oz and 4 lb 10 oz respectively. One fell to maggots, the other to a huge lobworm at only thirty yards range. But Martin and Steve who, wisely, had opted to fish the opposite swim on the other bank where they had seen a massive patch of bubbles early in the morning again had a terrific catch each. Martin took five fish with one of 5 lb 14 oz and Steve three, with one of 5 lb 10 oz. All the other fish were spawned out females of between 3 lb 8 oz and 4 lb 8 oz.

The average size of these tench, although still high, has dropped considerably due to the obvious spawning of the past few days. It will be interesting, therefore, to compare our catches again in a few days to see whether that really big one is still on the cards.

AFTERTHOUGHT

It is, perhaps, worth mentioning that, since the start of this new season, all my ledgering with the swim feeders has been with a fixed paternoster. During my close-season diving session I compared various ledger tackles and I was impressed by the simple paternoster. It has worked in practice very well indeed. Actual hooking feels more positive and the fact that the feeder is on a twelve-inch dropper and still in the water when I net a tench (instead of jiggling about out of the water and acting as a disgorger as with the running feeder) makes those last-minute lost fish a thing of the past.

I have found, though, that by joining two lengths of line with a blood knot and having the hook line from one of the droppers and with the feeder tied to the continuation of the knot, I get less tangles.

Monday, 21 and Tuesday, 22 June

Clammy, very warm evening and night — overcast at first but sunny from eight a.m. onwards.

I decided to fish for tench at the Marsh lake all through the night to see if feeding did, in fact, happen after dark.

On arrival yesterday evening at about eight I found fellow Broadland group member, Pete Stacey, already fishing as he had been from the early morning. Bites had been non-existent in the afternoon but he had hooked into six fish during the morning session, losing every one.

We discussed this while I tackled up and came to the conclusion that his rods were far too sloppy to set the hook well at distance. I showed him my tench-tamer rods which are basically $9^1/_2$ foot blanks of sportex thin-wall glass, but with a two-foot extension of fast-taper glass spigoted into the butt making $11^1/_2$ ft. all told. With these it is possible to hit into a tench at sixty yards and make it swirl on the surface.

As the light started to fade the tench came on in a brief spell of about an hour. I took one of 4 lb 8 oz and then Peter actually hooked into two at once. He handed the sloppy rod to me and concentrated on his mark 4 which had replaced the other. Peter netted a 4 lb 3 oz tench and, after giving my fish no quarter at all and virtually skitting it along the surface, I put it on the scales at 5 lb 3 oz. This was a pity — had Peter played and landed this one, it would have been his largest.

At midnight we realised that there would be no night-feeding cycle as such and put our heads down till dawn. The very minute the light started to poke through the clouds the tench started to pick up our maggots. I had just landed a plump $5^1/_4$ pounder when the bobbin shot up on the second rod and I added a 3 lb 10 oz male to the keepnet.

Then a peculiar thing happened: I lost a good fish which seemed to be fighting at twice its size. I inspected the hook which was good. Then the same thing happened again, but the fish did not come off. As the tench slid into the net I was aware of something following it and there, with its snout just inches from the frame, was a mean-looking large pike. It shot off upon seeing me but when I put the tench on to the scales I noticed that half its gill case was missing and there were bloody teeth marks all around its throat. The tench weighed 5 lb 4 oz. You don't really expect a 5 lb-plus tench to be grabbed during the fight — it really is quite a shock.

At six a.m., Martin and Steve arrived and moved in to our left. They made a very fortunate choice, for the tench quickly moved in front of them and two hours later Martin had five fish to 5 lb 10 oz and Steve, three to 4 lb.

How frustrating it is to leave this lake when the tench are still feeding. But so it goes.

Terry Houseago rang tonight and told me of his long awaited catch — I knew he would do it. On Sunday evening he caught nine tench in a mad, one-and-a-half-hour, feeding spell with no less than seven over 5 lb and the best 5 lb 10 oz — well done, Terry.

The author lifts a 5½lbs tench

Thursday, 24 June

Temperature well above 80° all day, very still.

I had intended to forget the tench for this evening's session and so I went along to a lake I know in North Norfolk which usually produces some nice rudd of $1^1/_2$ lb-plus. But the rudd must have been sleeping — unusual in very sunny weather — and the tench were feeding hard. As I approached the narrow shallow end of the lake at half past seven I could see the occasional disturbance between two thick weedbeds in fifteen inches of water. Occasionally a fin would surface and these I took to be rudd but, after setting up a rod on float tackle and creeping down to the lake edge, I immediately saw that they were, in fact, tench. They were milling about in twos and threes, sending up great clouds of bubbles. I catapulted a dozen or so pieces of flake and cast out into the nearest set of bubbles. Within minutes the float shot away and a really good fish shot out across the shallow bay. I was worried that my 3 lb line (put on with rudd in mind) would be insufficient to stop it before it made the first weed bed, but the hook pulled out and settled it for me.

I recast and missed an immediate 'flat'. I flicked the tackle straight out again and *bang* — off it shot. Result: a spawned-out female of around 3 lb. Not bad for starters, I thought, and although I had come for rudd I was enjoying myself. The next fish really churned up the bottom and weighed a shade over 4 lb. It was a beautiful textbook green colour quite different to the bigger fish of the Marsh lake which range from greeny brown to golden.

Unfortunately, those two fish must have affected the others and bites ceased, although I fished on for an hour. The light was starting to fade now and so I walked down to the dam end for a crack at the rudd. I groundbaited as usual and put two rods out with ledgered flake on both but, although I fished till midnight, not a bite did I have.

A nice evening, though.

Sunday, 27 June

Oppressively hot, temperature has been 80° plus for a week now, just a little wind.

Since the season started my five year old son Lee has been asking me to take him fishing, so this morning I woke him at 3 a.m. (he is keen and had his

65

clothes ready at the end of his bed) and took him off to the Marsh for some tenching.

This very warm weather usually sees the tench eager to feed but by five, after we had been fishing for over an hour in the company of Steve Harper and several other anglers scattered around the lake, not one bite had materialised. However, the ducks were diving well and three anglers including myself hooked into those frustrating shell ducks which have the nasty habit of picking up the maggots on the bottom in five feet of water.

When the sun started to break through at about six, I decided that perhaps our maggots had outlasted their effectiveness and I reeled in Lee's rod and changed the bait for a bunch of brandlings. Being a loose action rod which, like Lee, was incapable of hitting bites at sixty yards, I plopped it out ridiculously close to the bank in just two feet of water. Had it been any closer I could have seen the feeder on the bottom. After about ten minutes I saw the piece of silver paper, which I had folded over the line, slowly head towards the first ring. Although taken aback I instinctively grabbed for the rod, passed it over to Lee, and he was into his first big tench.

I yelled at him to keep the rod up, and told him when to stop winding when the bend on the rod looked nasty, but he played the fish very well indeed. The fish on 7 lb line was all but playing him, yet within two minutes there it was ready for the net — a nice female of 4 lb 13 oz.

He immediately said he wanted to catch another one and thinking that this was some kind of fluke I said I did not know about that. But after ten minutes up again went Lee's silver paper and another tench was on. This time he seemed to know what the game was all about and in a very short space of time a tench of 4 lb 15 oz was on its way to the keepnet.

Of course, Dad had now changed his baits to worm and was itching for some action, but up went Lee's silver paper again. This time, Lee reached the rod first and was standing up playing a 4 lb 8 oz tench before I opened my mouth.

Then Steve Harper hooked into something good at a distance which he said was not a tench. He was right, for after a really strong fight we could all see a massive perch fighting in the shallow, clear water towards Steve's net. It had taken a bunch of maggots intended for tench and looked as though it could have easily gone over the 3 lb mark, but in summer trim it took Steve's balance down to 2 lb 11½ oz. What a superb fish it was. I shall certainly do a spot of perching at this lake later on in the season as there appears to be a very excellent chance of a 3 lb-plus fish.

Shortly after this piece of excitement it was my turn for some action and, in a brief thirty-minute spell while casting to a particular spot some thirty yards further out than Lee's bait, I took three tench of 5 lb 6 oz, 5 lb 6 oz and 5 lb 3 oz. Then I lost a further two and it was Lee's turn for some more. All were taking the bunches of brandlings, sometimes tipped with a couple of maggots, sometimes on their own. But it was the worms the tench wanted. Lee added another three tench — the best of exactly 5 lb to the keepnet and I accounted for another two — both around the 4 lb 8 oz mark.

The young specimen hunter

When we decided to call it a day at lunchtime the tench were still feeding but less strongly. We hoisted the glistening net onto the grass for some photographs and I immediately noticed that one particular fish looked familiar; it was the very one that the pike had gnawed a few days previously — part of its gill missing and teeth wounds around the throat. Apparently it was none the worse for its ordeal of being hooked twice and bitten once all in the same week. I returned it and the others.

Lee and I watched them swim out into the lake until sunlight on the surface ruined our view, and I thought what a magnificent morning it had been. A really unforgettable fishing session and, I am certain, another specimen hunter in the making.

Tuesday, 29 June

Very misty until 6 o'clock and then hot bright sunshine with not a cloud in the sky.

Andy Jubb called for me early this morning, most eager to get among the big tench we have been catching. I assured Andy that he was bound to better his best tench but, as usual whenever I make these statements, we had a blank day. We had a few bites and missed them all, but Andy liked the water and fancies another crack so I shall take him again in a week or so.

The Marsh lake really is a moody water. It — or rather its tench — seem to know when an angler is fishing it for the first time, and so gives you a blank just to show that these big tench aren't quite so easy as all that.

Thursday, 1 July

Still very warm, slight easterly wind, bright sunshine from six a.m.

I popped along to the Marsh again this morning hoping that I might possibly hook into one of those big perch in addition to some tench.

From the moment I started fishing at 4 a.m., the tench were feeding and I took a nice brace of 5 lb 8$^1/_2$ oz and 5 lb during the first hour.

Brandlings are definitely a better bait now and, compared with maggots, the tench take them with far more confidence though small twitches before short runs are occurring. In fact, because the east wind came from behind me I was able to watch the line in a calm area close to the bank and see the twitches or the start of a bite long before the bobbin moved. If conditions were always like this the number of tench caught would easily be doubled.

I became quite obsessed with trying to beat the bobbin and took another two tench of 4 lb 2 oz and 4 lb 6 oz on very slight lifts of the line while the bobbin hung static. Each bite was preceded by two or three slight twitches of the line and then the slow lift. Whether the bobbin would eventually have lifted enough for me to see a hittable bite, I'm not certain, but several twitches and slow line lifts *not* followed by the bobbin flying up made me decide to hit the line twitches. The trouble with striking these small bites at a distance, especially when baiting with brandlings, is that quite often the tench has merely gripped them between its lips and not actually consumed them. In consequence, I find the ratio of fish to bites is very small indeed, frustratingly

Fixing the ledger bobbins

small. This morning I probably had around twenty-five bites for four fish. Oh, and a perch at last — $3^1/_2$ oz.

I am looking forward to a trip tomorrow morning when I intend to concentrate on watching the line and ignoring the bobbins — if the wind holds in the east.

Friday, 2 July

A still, misty morning followed by a slight east wind and bright sunshine.

I managed to rise early and, as planned, visited the Marsh. My decision of yesterday to hit the line lifts and twitches and ignore the ledger bobbins paid off to such an extent that I caught two tench from half-a-dozen bites. It's a pity that they were so few and far between because I felt quite confident when striking at the slightest nibble. The tench weighed 4 lb 14 oz (female) and 3 lb 14 oz (male).

I think I shall leave the lake for a while to give the tench a rest from my continual fishing in the hope that more bites might result. I hope when I return that the growth of blanket weed, caused by the continual sunshine, has not become thicker. For the past four sessions huge clumps have clung to the terminal tackle on the retrieve. Worse still are the layers growing up to the surface between rod and bait. As the line must rest in several places on the weed it is no wonder that bites are mere twitches, due to the resistance a biting fish feels. We need some rain and plenty of it but, as I look outside, the sun still beats down without a cloud in the sky. I cannot remember such a long period of high temperatures before.

Saturday, 3 July

Very warm night without a hint of mist, sunny morning.

My wife Barbara and I spent a very pleasant evening and all-night session at Gunton Park lake after the bream in the company of Nobby and Maureen Clarke.

We decided beforehand to make it a lighthearted competition ending with a fry-up breakfast at the lakeside. After concentrating all through the night we had little to show for our efforts. The fish were particularly finicky and bites rather spasmodic all night through. I lost two fish on the strike and landed two of 5 lb 4 oz and 4 lb 2 oz. Nobby had just one of 4 lb 6 oz in his net. It was a most relaxed and interesting trip despite the lack of action and after breakfast, when the fishing petered out and we were all on the point of packing up, a friendly mole which Nobby had seen moving about at this spot before became quite inquisitive.

The mole kept burrowing up through the soft marginal growth at various points to look at us. I took a couple of lobworms from the tin and, on all fours, crept quietly up to see if I could feed him. I must have looked a bit touched to the other anglers around the lake, crouched on dry land holding a worm out to some invisible being, especially as Nobby was two feet away clicking away with the camera. But that little mole really made my day when he popped up, pushed a long pink snout towards me, and snatched the worm. I immediately tried another worm and it was taken in a flash. Barbara then passed over the maggot tin with a pair of forceps and I tried to tease him out of the hole by offering a bunch of maggots. I could feel him munching on the maggots at the end of the forceps and slowly eased him up out of his hole. What a pretty little fellow he was, too. He had squinty little eyes hidden between thin strands of lightish fur and a pinkish snout — pig-like but much longer than I had imagined. The front paws with tiny fingers and sharp claws seemed unlikely to be responsible for the digging that moles do. I fed him about a quarter-pint of maggots before he was full and went down below to get on with his burrowing.

A beautiful fishing trip thanks to our mole, two bream, a fried breakfast, and good company.

Monday, 5 July

Still warm and sunny.

Peter Stacey rang yesterday evening with news of a one-acre lake that a farmer friend had to let which had been stocked with fifty mirror and leather carp some four years ago. Peter was very excited at the prospect of our specimen group acquiring the water, and all we had to do was take a look and say yes or no.

So this evening together with Dickie, Chris and Steve, I drove south to the village of Tacolneston and then along some winding lanes to a remote spot where we had arranged to meet Peter. He had given me a map reference and we easily found the meeting place. Peter arrived shortly and we quickly made our way across a couple of meadows to a small and secluded lake. It was about an acre all told and roughly circular, with a narrow neck at one end. Two small islands close together in the centre added visual interest and, with dense patches of broad leaf potamageton pond weed on the surface and mountains of curly pond weed down below, it certainly looked a rich water.

Peter had been doing a bit of fish spotting earlier and had seen between ten and twenty large carp. He would not commit himself on this because the lake was very coloured and to gauge a fish's size was difficult. We had taken some bread along and, within minutes of lobbing in some crusts, Dickie saw one double-figure fish swirl for one and another, of about 8 lb, suck in a piece as soon as it hit the water. He also saw a small mirror of about 12 oz roll, which is encouraging because the farmer stocked the lake with 2 lb fish. They are obviously breeding.

We had soon seen enough and went along to pay the farmer our fee for the year and to arrange a lease. The lake is just what we have been looking for and, with such an established carp stock, it should produce some excellent sport in the future.

I am going to rise early in the morning and have a crack at the open clearing where Dickie saw the carp suck in his crusts. I just cannot wait.

Terry Houseago rang later this evening and told me of his trip to Gunton lake on Sunday evening through to Monday morning. He fished the same swim as did Nobby and me on Saturday night and took twenty-one bream to 5 lb 4 oz. He caught them really close in and on our tench tactics of swim feeder and maggots — why didn't I try that!

Tuesday, 6 July

Warm morning, quite dull till six o'clock when sunshine broke through.

I woke at three and, tingling with anticipation, drove towards our new carp lake to be there for daybreak. I arrived a bit late but still with four hours fishing before work. How I love these long summer mornings.

After parking the car, I scrambled through the barbed-wire fence (we shall have to put a stile here) and walked slowly round the lake. All seemed quiet when suddenly a carp started to wallow and suck on the surface in the very

The carp lake

clearing where I had planned on fishing. Trying not to make too much noise I skirted the swim and came up from behind it through tall nettles and weeds (most uncomfortable, but at least I won't have to crunch them down next time). I put up two rods — both tench tamers with 9 lb line and size 2 Lion d'Or hooks — the best hooks I have ever used. One rod would fish freelined a huge lump of flake and the other would be at the ready with a crust for anything moving on the surface. After making up the landing net I grabbed the loaf and, leaving my tackle bag well back from the water's edge, moved stealthily forwards, breaking off nettle stems as I went to give me a yard-wide gap for casting and playing.

It was a great feeling, to know that neither these carp nor, indeed, the lake itself had ever been fished before.

Almost before I had decided where to cast the flake a nice fish showed on the surface to my left. I picked up the other rod, dunked the crust at my feet, and flicked it a yard beyond the last swirl. The fish moved towards it and sucked the crust down slowly and confidently. I saw the line tighten across the surface and then set the hook as hard as I dared. The carp wondered what had happened for a few seconds and came speeding across the surface towards me (the water cannot be much more than two feet deep anywhere), and then turned to my right into a thick bed of the broad leaf weed, the type with nasty tough stems. It went plunging through for several feet before I managed to pull it back out again, and then shot off to the other side of the clearing and buried itself. I kept heaving, with the line near to breaking point, and after several minutes the fish freed itself and came grudgingly towards the waiting net. A lovely mirror in mint condition and pulling the balance down to 9 lb 13 oz.

During the following three hours I experienced some wonderful sport. Each fish I hooked fought as hard as the first and one particular leather, at 6 lb 10 oz the smallest fish, actually leapt clear of the water no less than six times within the first twenty seconds of hooking it. In fact, all the fish (and I had another three of 7 lb 13 oz, 9 lb, and 9 lb 7 oz) fought incredibly strongly. I was amazed at their power and my inability to stop them on fairly stout tackle from crashing into the weed. All but the first took freelined flake (nothing surfaced after the first fish except some annoying canadian geese which will definitely have to go). I missed three good bites and pulled out of two more carp, losing a third in the weed. It was so heavily buried that I pulled for a break after twenty minutes. I rather fancy that the fish had long since departed, anyway.

A clean mirror carp of 9lbs 13oz

It was a terrific start to what is obviously going to be a magnificent group water. With a fairly good growth weight, and accepting that the fish I took this morning were the norm for those fish introduced at 2 lb just four years ago, we should be in for some even more exciting fishing yet.

Thursday, 8 July

Still very very warm and sunny from six a.m., when will this weather break?

I visited our new carp lake again this morning and fished from 3.30 a.m. until nine o'clock. It was a particularly interesting session and in complete contrast to my first trip when all the fish I caught and hooked were of good size. This morning's catch consisted of all small ones, except for one.

I started at the spot I call the slope because of the high gradient down to the water, where I caught all the fish on Tuesday. After a frustrating hour of missing seemingly good runs, I finally hooked one of the culprits, — a 1 lb 8 oz mirror. Six others like it and a 1 lb 8 oz tench were to follow in rapid succession. Then, because there seemed no end to these small fish, I took a walk with just the net and rods to the other side of the lake to see if anything was moving.

Where the end of the lake finishes in a funnel between overhanging brambles, with thick surface weed all along the margins, I found a small clearing and plopped out two baits some five yards apart, both as near the marginal weed as I could.

A little while later a hump, followed by a big tail, appeared a few feet from my nearest bait. Then, just seconds later, the line hissed through the water as the fish bolted back into the weed. I struck smartly and heaved all in one go. A goodish fish boiled in the weed and sped out into the clearing, only to plunge straight into more weed to my right. I managed to stop it from going too far and then out it came again, but right back into the weed where I had first hooked it. After a real tug-of-war for several minutes as much with the weed as with the carp, I netted a lovely mirror of 9 lb 2 oz. 9 lb seems to be a common weight for the larger fish here. The next bite I missed, and the next. Then I connected with a really hefty fish, certainly into double figures, which was bent on not returning from its first run deep into the weed, so I put everything on and promptly straightened the hook.

All went quiet for about an hour and then, with just a few minutes to go before it was time to head for work, I took a baby mirror of 1 lb 4 oz. There really seems no end to these small fellows. It is obviously such a fertile lake that the occupants can not stop breeding, and I rather fear that before long we are going to have to do a netting job to remove the surplus young fish. For the time being, we are, however, putting all the small fellows under 2 lb into a tiny pond adjacent to the lake. It is actually joined by a narrow dyke and when the water level returns to its norm (the lake is two feet down at present) I think we shall need to stake the entrance to stop the carp swimming from one to the other.

Sunday, 11 July

Very warm night, bright sunshine from six a.m.

I have just returned from an all-night carping session which started at eight p.m. yesterday and finished twelve hours later this morning. It was a particularly enjoyable trip, not so much because of the fish we caught but because Vic Bellars and I finally got together at his favourite water near Swaffham in West Norfolk, something we had been planning for over a year now. Vic has this obsession with being at one with nature and, to this end has painted every single piece of his angling gear olive — camouflage green. Not only is the usual stuff, such as rods, umbrellas, bite alarms, stools, etc., greened over, but also sundries like the water container, kettle, food box and gas stove. This morning I noticed that he has even painted his forceps green and, when I came to do the washing up, even the scouring brush (you've guessed it) — green.

Vic is also keen on fishing in comfort. When we arrived at the lake last night the first item he pulled out of the car was his commissariat box, as he calls it. Inside was mountains of food, choice of tea or coffee, and all the cooking and washing-up utensils required. Luckily, we only had to carry his box of goodies (a 3 ft × 2 ft crate) a few yards to his swim. We unpacked the rest of our gear and Vic showed me the swim he had baited up with special cheese flavoured baits that I was to fish. It was an attractive spot, with three small islands some twenty yards out.

I could easily imagine the route that patrolling carp would take around these islands which were mostly overgrown with shrub alders whose branches hung well into the water. Vic's swim was to my right and directly opposite the end island; he then had an open bay and, further to his right, a small island

Vic Bellars with commissariat

close to the bank, festooned with brambles and branches reaching into the lake. In all, a snaggy but very carpy water of some two acres.

Vic had fished these swims before with success and suggested that my best cast would be a long one between the end and middle island, over a gravel bar which was clearly visible and into five feet of water on the other side. Unfortunately, the trees grew overhead from one island to the other so that I was almost casting into a tunnel. Luckily, apart from casting into the trees on my first attempt, I spent the rest of the night without snarl-ups.

All went very slowly until about one a.m., with the full moon out and unusually warm. Then the silver paper on my left rod shot up and I found myself into a mirror carp: not a big one but quite scrappy in such a snaggy lake and which pulled the balance to 8 lb 6 oz. I cast out again and had an instant take again from the spot over the gravel bar, which I missed. After this, the swim became infested with small tench and bream. They twitched and knocked the bait about for a couple of hours, during which time I actually caught a tench and a bream of about a pound each on a size 2 hook.

Then all went quiet again, and I waited for dawn and some carp to move. Just before sun-up, I heard crashing and a slipping clutch zinging away from Vic's swim and then a loud curse as he parted company with a good fish which, he later told me, had tried to go round the middle island and succeeded. A short while later, I heard some more crashing about and a shout from Vic that he had a mirror of 9 lb in the net.

Not to be outdone, I got stuck into another mirror of 8 lb 14 oz which was incredibly long and which went so hard that had I lost it I would have guessed to be twice that weight. The trouble with fishing obstacle-course carp lakes is that every fish seems to make for the nearest snag. In consequence you pull harder, and then so does the carp and, before long, you imagine it to be much bigger that it really is.

Within an hour of dawn breaking the sun was so bright that we both knew sport was over. Vic then gave me a conducted tour of the lake and told me of some big bream which live here. He has taken them to 8 lb — plus in the past and I suspect that we shall have a trip after them a little later on when the little tench won't be so eager for food.

The author with a mirror carp

Tuesday, 13 July

Muggy morning, sun finally breaking through at eight a.m., still very warm.

I went along to our carp water this morning at three for an early session before work, but I may as well not have bothered. This continual tropical weather has evaporated a good six inches of water since I fished here last week, and now most of the lake is under two feet deep. In consequence, very little appears to be moving except, of course, the tiny mirrors. Dickie and Peter were also fishing and they, too, were without a decent carp run. Nevertheless, we did manage to account for eight little fellows $1\frac{1}{2}$ lb — all on size 2 hooks, which we transferred to the stock pond.

I intend to give the lake a rest for at least a fortnight or until we have some rain to liven things up, and I rather fancy a spot of chubbing or breaming.

Friday, 16 July

Warm evening, clear sky, misty after dark.

Yesterday, the long awaited rain finally decided to fall, and quite a storm it was, too. I was out after dark collecting worms from the lawn which needed the rain almost as much as the local rivers do. By this evening, however, the sky had cleared again and I decided on the spur of the moment to take my son, Lee, fishing for a few hours to Gunton Lake.

My usual swim was taken so we walked along some fifty yards and nestled in between the rushes. We tried for the bream until about eleven when, with no fish in the net, I decided to call it a night.

AFTERTHOUGHT

I have decided to take the bream seriously from next week and have booked a trip to Broadlands Lake for Monday evening. It is boat fishing only and I have made a set of special rod rests, which clamp onto the gunwhale, and reach into the centre of the boat with two U rests to take the rod butts. Two separate heads each on its own G clamp go on the transom. This will enable me to fish down the whole length of the boat facing the after end so I can get a full sweep on the strike. I fished for the bream at this particular lake last season but had trouble hitting the bites. It is so shallow that casting some forty yards to the ground bait is necessary.

Whether my rod rest idea will help the number of bites hit to those missed remains to be seen. I shall certainly be fishing with the paternoster terminal rig which I have been using ever since my diving session during the close season. I found it very good when hitting the tench at distance at the Marsh lake, and I see no reason why it should not be as effective with big bream. I have taken them from Broadlands to nearly six pounds which, compared with some that live there, are only tiddlers. I lost one, estimated at nine pounds — plus last September, and that's the figure I am aiming for.

Special boat rod rests

F

Monday, 19 July

Fresh SW winds, rain from two a.m. until five.

I visited Broadlands Lake last night with good but very mixed results. Arriving at eight p.m., I left the boat dyke, which lies at the northern end of this long water, and veered right towards the southern end where a small island is situated in the centre. At this point, which is the widest, the bottom shelves from eighteen inches at one bank to three and a half feet at the other over a distance of some two hundred yards. This deeper bank, lined with tall reeds, is the favourite location for tench which patrol along the fringes. In the middle, just off the small island, is my favourite pitch; I don't know why, because the depth here, about four feet, is the same throughout the middle of the lake.

The water was coloured and looked very fishy, with small fry and the occasional good fish churning the surface. I put the pole in at each end of the boat, tied up and then put the rods together. I used the faithful tench-tamers (so good for picking up line) with six-pound test and size 6 hooks on the paternosters. The rods fitted quite well in the boat rests but the front rests were a little high and kept too much line out of the water.

Half an hour before darkness fell I untied the boat and paddled quietly out some thirty yards to put the ground bait down: four loaves mixed with 7 lb of rusk. It's so much easier just easing it over the side than throwing it. I don't think rowing over the swim disturbs it either because, as soon as I was tied up at the poles again and put the bread flake baits out, the bream moved in. It was dark now and the isotope bobbins showed up beautifully, despite the yawing of the boat. Bites were really positive — straight up to the butt ring, but I missed nine in a row. Then I felt that satisfying, heavy thump of a good bream on the end. It kited round some thirty yards to my left and I slowly made ground. It seemed a very good fish, indeed, and after several attempts at netting it behind the boat, with quite a chop on the surface, I finally lifted out a really long fish. I was overjoyed, guessing a weight of over 8 lb — and I was right! There, in torchlight, was a pike of about 9 lb hooked well inside the jaws. How I hate these flake-munching pike!

I settled in again and, after several missed bites, I finally managed to foul hook a bream of about 5 lb in the dorsal fin. I felt the hook snag on the retrieve, when I was about half way in, so I had obviously been overcasting; a common occurrence at night.

After this episode I started to connect at a reduced range. A drop bite resulted in a very long tench of about 4 lb which I did not weigh and certainly did not expect whilst seeking the bream. But the next bite — the usual sail-away lift of the bobbin — resulted in one of the fellows I was after. This fish went quite well, kiting first to the left and then to the right and finally ending up behind the boat where I put the net under an apparently big bream. I thought at first that it might go over the 8 lb mark, but it was thin, a male with tiny white tubicles still left on its nose from spawning. It pulled the scales down to 7 lb 9 oz, which was good enough.

I really seemed to be getting the groundbait range at last and, for over an hour, I could expect a bite on either rod within a couple of minutes of casting. But could I hit them? This problem arises so often with big bream that I no longer worry about it. After at least a dozen good lifts I connected again. This was a smaller fish but quite scrappy and, at 5 lb 12 oz, most welcome. Like the previous one it could have weighed a pound heavier for its size but I suppose they have not long spawned and have yet to reach their peak.

At exactly two o'clock, just when I was feeling cocky and expecting to take several more, there was a heavy rustle from over the trees behind me. Within minutes a strong wind blew up accompanied by rain and up went the brolly. I sat there for about an hour watching the bobbins jingling about, first at the butt ring and then on the deck, and I realised that I had two choices: either I sat it out in the hope that the rain cleared with the chance of some more sport or I snatched some much-needed sleep. I decided on the latter. I should have liked to stay but we need rain so badly that I cannot be too sorry about it. I have booked another trip for Thursday evening.

Friday, 23 July

Overcast but with long clear periods throughout the night, quite mild, slight NW wind.

As planned I made an early start yesterday evening and was on Broadlands Lake by eight-thirty. Luckily, the overcast weather failed to produce rain even though the wind dropped as darkness fell. I hate all night sessions when it rains most of the time, especially thunder with lightening. This time the weather and condition of the water were both perfect, but the bream were extremely cagey.

I ledgered flake as usual on both rods and had to wait till about ten-thirty for the first bite which, I promptly dealt with by snapping off. I cannot think how this happened as it is difficult enough to hook these bream let alone hit them hard enough to break the line.

I hit the second bite and subsequently landed a bream of just under 5 lb. Then I started to miss bite after bite. I am quite used to this happening with bream; if there is anything on the end when I sweep into a powerful strike once the bobbin has reached the butt ring I treat it as a bonus. The bream fed spasmodically from ten-thirty p.m. until around two thirty a.m. Throughout this period I found it extremely difficult to locate the shoal, which was seldom over the groundbait and, when bites in a particular spot ceased, I had to cast all over the place till I found them again. The second fish was a bream of about 2 lb 8 oz which I somehow managed to lasso around the middle. The third, and last, bream weighed 5 lb 3 oz. I may have taken several more which came unstuck on the strike, as did something that I hooked which proved a stalemate: an eel, no doubt, so its just as well the hook came out.

As dawn broke I realised that to continue for the bream was a waste of time and so I moved position over to the eastern bank where the tench love to patrol along the huge beds of bulrushes. I put the poles down about twenty yards from the rushes and, keeping the same baits and terminal rigs, I cast them out as close to the reed fringe as I dared. Then I catapulted out a dozen pieces of bait-sized flake and sat back. A little while later, before I had started to feel the effects of being up all night, the left hand bobbin shot up and I missed it. A cloud of bubbles shot up to the surface where the tench had been.

Half an hour later I had another run on the right hand bobbin and, this time I connected with a very long male tench, bent on crashing headlong into the rushes. I soon bullied him out again and into the net at 4 lb 8 oz — a big tench for a male. After this excitement, I had no sooner recast than the bobbin went zooming up again for a scrappy male tench, 2 oz lighter than the first. A lovely brace of powerful fish. Those spoon-shaped pelvic fins of the male tench seem to give him such an aggressive look and, of course, they always fight much harder than the female. I fished on till seven thirty without another bite and then made for work.

Wednesday evening should be interesting: Vic Bellars is taking me to his carp lake near Swaffham again, a water I would never tire of fishing, so it's back to carp for this week. From then on, for at least a month, I shall definitely concentrate on big bream.

Sunday, 25 July

Warm evening, just a little dawn mist followed by moderate northerly winds.

This morning I took up Charles Clay's offer to fish with him at a secluded, private lake near Fakenham, set in the beautiful grounds of a National Trust property. Whenever I am offered some sport on a potentially good water which I have never fished before I always expect to catch nothing. But this morning we actually caught some tench.

The lake is large (some ten acres) and, for the most part, very shallow with just one deep area at the outlet end where we fished from wooden staging. Charlie fished on the staging itself with a depth of about eleven feet at his rod tip. He put in some maggots and a little groundbait and decided to float-fish on the bottom for the tench which were bubbling away. I fished a little to his left from the rocky shore, over a large bed of potomogeten broadleaf weed, putting out two rods with freelined lobs on each. There were one or two tench bubbling about quite close in so that when one of my lines twitched and shot off I was surprised to find I had got a perch. Three perch later, between 6 and 12 oz I changed over to flake but without success. By now Charlie had enticed a huge tench shoal into his swim and had taken a couple around the 3 lb 8 oz mark.

I decided to walk round the lake and set off through the wooded undergrowth for the far end. I passed plenty of game on the way including a lovely young deer which stalked me for a few yards and then shot away as I adjusted the camera lens.

Most of the lake seemed so shallow (from six to twenty inches deep) that we were obviously fishing the best spot, so I made my way back. Bubbles were still coming up in Charlie's swim but his size 8 hook with a bunch of maggots was not producing. They came up sucked dry each time so I suggested that he shorten his bottom weight from eighteen inches to just four inches from the hook and change down to a size 12 hook holding three maggots only. This change produced four more tench and, as I sat on the staging beside him, I thought I might as well have a go myself. I picked up Charlie's spare rod and changed the hook to a size 14 with two maggots. This produced three tench before the bubbles stopped and we started to be pestered by six-inch roach. As they are excellent perch bait I popped one out on a tiny float with a size 4 hook in its top lip to see what was about. Minutes later the float shot off and I reeled in a 12 oz perch.

Charlie Clay's catch of tench

After this I lost interest somewhat and started taking a few photographs of the lake and of Charlie with the tench. We had nine to 4 lb 10 oz — not bad at all. I would certainly like to fish this lake again sometime. Though how to separate the small perch from the bigger ones which must surely exist would be a problem.

Tuesday, 27 July

Misty morning, no wind, sunny from six a.m.

Sid Johnson rang yesterday evening and asked where we were going in the morning. He is a professional diver, often away from home, so that when he does finally get a few day's leave I always try to organise a spur-of-the-moment trip. I was at a loss at first as to where to take him, but then I thought of the Waveney and the fact that so far this year I have not been chubbing, and at half past three this morning we set off.

We fished the river at Earsham where the main course of this beautiful river divides into several narrow dykes, all full of chub and big roach, but excessively weedy. I pointed out several chub swims to Sid upstream of the mill bridge and told him I was walking off down river to have a crack at some big roach I had seen there some while back. I crept cautiously up to several inviting swims where weed rafts lined the opposite bank, but one small chub, of about 2 lb, was all that looked at my freelined flake. I put him back and made for the swim where the big roach live. It is funnel-shaped, formed by bushes and weed rafts on both banks and finishing in a large weed raft covering the entire width of the river at the downstream end. Beneath it, close to the bottom in five feet of water, live about thirty roach ranging from a pound up to $2^1/_2$ lb.

I sat there for a few minutes flicking in a piece of flake every thirty seconds and then put my hook in a piece. The line went slack as the flake reached the bottom and then immediately tightened on a roach of about $1^1/_4$ lb. I put him back, well upstream, and tried again. This time I had a tiny one of 12 oz and then another of just over the pound. Then all went dead as the light came upon the clear water.

I had a few casts into various swims and holes in the weed on my way upstream again and took a chub of $2^3/_4$ lb on a twitched lob. When I reached the mill bridge Sid was back again (after a walk upriver) at the first swim and, by the look of his rod, into a good fish. I hurried up with the net and slipped it under his biggest chub to date: a long fish of 4 lb $^1/_2$ oz which would if it had been in better shape, have come closer to the 5 lb mark. It accepted freelined flake in a narrow run between the streamer weed and put a smile on Sid's face.

Sid Johnson with a good chub

Thursday, 29 July

Clear sky all night and subsequently very cold from around midnight till dawn, strong sunshine cleared the mist.

I have just returned from an all-night carping session in the company of Vic Bellars. He arranged for us to fish the lake near Swaffham which proved productive two weeks ago but this time the conditions were against us. Only the myriad small tench, which cannot get onto the baits quick enough, were active. I took four around 2 lb apiece on balls of cheese-flavoured paste larger than a chicken's egg. My one piece of excitement throughout the night was when I switched on the torch to see a large water vole standing up on its hind legs in three inches of water biting its way through the mesh of my landing net. Vic fared even worse than me. He did not have any rats caught up in his net because it remained dry all night. He did not have a single twitch.

I left him at seven-thirty a.m., still daring his bobbins to move, and started the forty-mile drive to Norwich and to work. Back to the bream next time — at least they bite all night even if I cannot hook them.

Tuesday, 3 August

Coolish night, NW winds varying from very light to fresh, overcast with the promise of rain.

I have just returned from an all night breaming stint on Broadlands Lake where, although I failed to take one of the specimen 7 lb — plus bream, a mixed bag comprising two roach, one pike, three ducks and six bream was quite interesting, to say the least.

I was not very optimistic when I rowed onto the lake at eight p.m. yesterday evening because the wind was very strong and the thought of sitting the night out with a good chance of some heavy rain did not appeal. I like to see the bream bow waving along the surface at dusk so that, when I put the groundbait down, I know it won't be long before they move into the swim. But there was absolutely nothing moving at all and until about half past ten my ledger bobbins remained motionless. Then the wind eased a little and I had a bite: the first duck. How on earth the little blighters manage to find a piece of flake, amongst the silt and weed on the bottom in the dark in such coloured water, amazes me; but they do. Luckily, though, this one, like the two others I caught later, was bill hooked and was none the worse for its greediness.

Shortly afterwards I caught the first bream, about 5 lb, hooked through its dorsal fin. In such shallow water foul hooking is common-place and often, throughout the night when fishing here, I feel a clunk as either the hook or bomb touches a fish. The second bream was about the same weight and so was the third — both neatly hooked through the bottom lip and taking the isotope bobbin right up to the butt ring.

Until now, I had been using 10 lb braided dacron on one of the rods and the usual 6 lb bayer on the other. This was in the hope of more bites but, as I had no bites whatsoever on the dacron rod, I could not find out. I changed over the spool to mono again and, curiously, I then had bites on both. I could not see why no bites were forthcoming on the dacron. It is only a little thicker than the 6 lb mono and, in any event, I used a mono hook length. I intend trying it again for I am certain that, with its no-stretch properties, I would hit more bites.

To be honest, though, after those three bream bites were few and far between. I thought, after hitting into a real tearaway bite, that I had finally hooked a big bream but, after playing it carefully for several minutes and bringing it up to the net, I realised that another pike had taken a liking for flake — a lean fish of about 7 lb.

In the period just before dawn I had a series of reasonable bites but they were from small fish: Roach to 14 oz and bream $2^1/_2$ lb. Only one fish was better than these and, stupidly, I tried to bully it in. The inevitable happened, the hook pulling out as the bream made a huge boil on the surface.

By five-thirty bites had faded away to nothing and I did not like the look of the sky. Almost half the lake was covered in a curtain of grey, warning of certain rain. I packed up the rods, shipped the mooring poles, and rowed back to the boathouse. Halfway in I was treated to the beautiful sight of the sun fighting to force its way through the heavy clouds whilst the rain bucketed down across one half of the lake. Behind the trees, high up in the sky, was the brightest, most colourful, rainbow I think I have ever seen.

AFTERTHOUGHT

On the results of these past trips to the lake, it would appear that the best chance of the bigger bream lies between the hours of ten p.m. and two a.m., and that there is an enormous head of 5 lb fish between the angler and real heavies.

If bites are prolific on my next trip I feel fairly certain now of hitting a good proportion. I am consciously keeping the rod low and striking sideways which picks up the line far quicker than a hurried upwards sweep. My tally of twelve fish from about thirty-six bites is the best yet — even if three of them *were* ducks.

Flake still remains a good taking bait in conjunction with the bucket of mashed bread and rusk groundbait I put in at the start of the session. I have periodically switched over during the last three sessions to maggots on smaller hooks but without bites so, unless the bream become really suspicious of bread, I shall stay with flake on size 6 hooks.

Thursday, 5 August

A very overcast and still night.

Terry Houseago and I fished my favourite location — Broadlands Lake — to see if we could get among those big bream and, fortunately, did just that. Our catch also included a perch, a pike, a roach, three tench and a duck, in addition to seven bream, all on breadflake. I never quite know just what is going to grab the bait next.

We started at dusk by rowing quietly out to my usual spot in the middle putting down the groundbait. We fished in separate boats in the hope that tangles during the night could be avoided. We should have known better: Terry's first bite was a duck which insisted on going under my boat and taking both my lines with it. Once the duck had been unhooked and put back, to grab our flake another day, we started to get some bites from bream. But unlike those of my previous three trips, when I experienced countless, positive bites with the bobbin shooting right up the butt ring, these were tiny twitches followed by a three or four-inch lift. We could not understand this, for the weather and water conditions were near to perfection. The night was warm and overcast with absolutely no wind on the surface.

We persevered, trying to hit these finicky bites and, eventually, I managed to latch onto what seemed like a very large bream. But, from past experience here, I should have known that pike fight like big bream and, after a careful fight lasting several minutes, a 10 lb 7 oz pike lay in the bottom on my landing net. What a letdown! Terry was doing likewise in his area to the left of mine. He had three hits in a row, all tench between $3^1/_2$ lb and $4^3/_4$ lb. Then I hit an immediate take and wound in a 6 oz roach, quickly followed by a six-inch perch, all on flake. We were puzzled by our mixed bag and began to wonder if there were, in fact, any bream at all over our groundbait.

From about midnight to two a.m., bites were spasmodic and those we had we could not hit. I tried casting way beyond the groundbait and instantly located a nice bream of just under 6 lb. This encouraged us a little and Terry soon followed suit by hitting into a big one which boiled heavily on the surface as he struck and continued to fight hard all the way in. He immediately put it on the scales which registered 7 lb 5 oz — a personal best.

We were quite hopeful now even though on previous trips only the smaller bream have been evident at this time of day. We fished on without another bite, until the light was good enough for us to see what a mess the boat was in

Terry Houseago and the author with bream, tench and pike

— mud, bread and groundbait slopping about everywhere. Although the sky was still overcast I imagined that our sport was over. Then I noticed several goodish fish roll to my right, some fifty yards from our baited area. I swapped the $^1/_4$ oz arlesey bomb for a one ounce and threw a bait close to the swirl.

I clipped the bobbin onto the line and sat back, only to see it fly straight up to the butt ring. I struck immediately and a big bream rolled and crashed on the surface taking a few yards from the reel at the same time. I knew it was another big one and I was right — 7 lb 1 oz exactly. I put the flake out to the same area again and up went the bobbin. This one weighed 5 lb 8 oz. The next was 5 lb 7 oz and then a four-pounder followed by a baby of one pound.

During this hectic spell, which should not really have happened, Terry sat watching motionless bobbins. It seemed that the bream had long since left our baited area and, as I was casting well over to my right with Terry's boat to my left, it was impossible for Terry to reach the same area.

Just why the bream were lying in this particular spot puzzled me for it is no deeper than anywhere else. However, on my next visit, I shall position the boat to cover this patch, and my usual spot, by mooring some thirty yards to the right. Perhaps they will be more inclined to feed well at night there, perhaps not, or maybe I shall find them in the usual spot. We shall see.

An entertaining night's fishing, full of surprises, and with a couple of specimens thrown in. What more can one ask.

Monday 9th August

Overcast evening — clear night — with very light N/E wind — mild.

If I was fortunate enough to be granted just one wish, it would be that I might finally solve the soul-destroying problem of not being able to hit those slow-positive bream bites I have been getting lately. Last night I must have missed at least twenty good bites, pricked three and netted just three fish: hours of ridiculous frustration which, needless to say, happened at Broadlands lake.

I could not resist another visit, this time in the company of Kevin Dawson with whom I had fished for the tench at the Marsh Lake in June.

Kevin wanting to have a crack at the big bream, we left the boat house yesterday evening at about eight and made straight for the area where I took fish last Thursday. Although quite windy and cloudy to start with, the conditions soon changed. From 10 am, when the bites started in earnest, the wind very quickly dropped to a flat calm and the sky cleared, showing the brightest full moon I have ever fished under.

After having missed all the early bites, we assumed that the moon would drop the temperature and put the bream off. But no – the night was really quite warm – and the bream fed on until around 3.30 am. The bites came in short bursts of two or three quite positive lifts of the bobbin from a particular spot within our baited area; and then the fish would move on.

We soon got on to this pattern and kept casting around if a bite was not forthcoming within say ten minutes. Kevin was first to draw blood, a little after midnight, with a tench of 4lbs. Then I hit a bite just like all the others I had missed and actually connected with a very good bream, but only for a few seconds. Kevin's line must have been over mine and he struck what he thought was a bite, knocking my fish off the hook.

A little later I connected with another and the hook was obviously well home as a big bream welled heavily on the surface some forty yards out: a beautiful sight in the moonlight. I pumped it in carefully and put the net under another seven pounder (7lbs 3oz to be precise). There really does seem to be an excellent head of big bream on the lake. But, unfortunately, there was nothing like it to follow. I missed several more sure bites, caught one small bream of about 2lbs and a male tench of around 4lbs. The tench bites I just cannot miss. The bobbin always zooms up to the rod butt; I think the rod would go in if I didn't strike.

Kevin accounted for another tench of $3^1/_2$lbs, a bream of $4^3/_4$lbs and, like me, missed countless, seemingly unmissable, slow bream bites.

I shall have to put on my thinking cap again and get to the bottom of these missed bites. I fancy trying the dacron again and, perhaps, much larger baits on big hooks – 2's and 4's. I used soft bread paste last night instead of flake to good effect (bite wise at least). Perhaps, by switching over to maggots in conjunction with a swim feeder, I might do better, although the splash of its entry in such shallow water might have the reverse effect, and I shall leave these tactics to the very last. One particular aspect I have considered all along in trying to hit more bites is to pull the line through the water by striking low to the surface. To strike upwards creates excessive drag on the strike, as the line lifts up against the surface tension.

Naturally, I always point the rods at the bait, with the tips low to the surface, so that a biting fish feels the least amount of resistance. But – and this may very well be the missed bite answer – as I strike sideways, with the line pointing at the fish, I must move the angle of line sideways through the water in alignment with the rod tip. As my tench-tamers are $11^1/_2$ feet long, I move that line at least a couple of feet sideways through the water before the hook goes home – or doesn't.

On my next visit, both rods will be arranged at an angle to the line, so that when I strike I follow through without the line deviating at all. This method will perhaps make for less bites as fish are bound to feel resistance from the rod tip prior to pulling the bobbin up.

But it is the only thing I can think of in yet another attempt to beat the bream.

Friday, 13 August

No wind, a calm misty night.

I visited Broadlands Lake, and the bream, yet again yesterday evening, with a view to staying all night but the weather conditions were all against it and I was back home in bed by two o'clock this morning.

As darkness fell over the lake I expected bites as usual but, within minutes, a thick mist rolled across the water keeping the bream very quiet. I think I had just four good bites in four hours. I tried the dacron again, some fine 6 lb stuff which I managed to snap on the very first bite. I switched over to mono on both rods and connected almost immediately with a good bream which, unfortunately, came adrift after about twenty seconds. Then I netted a tench of $4^3/_4$ lb and missed another bite.

Not a good evening, but I am sure only the conditions stopped the bream from moving. Shallow lakes always seem to fish poorly when shrouded in mist.

Sunday, 15 August

Misty, still night followed by hot sunshine, heatwave conditions again.

Colin Froude who, because he lives so far away, seldom fishes with me these days, rang a few weeks ago to arrange last night's breaming session. We had decided to have a go at "the Conifers" Lake where a great deal of my winter is spent after the numerous pike. Having known about its prolific bream stock for some while, I thought it was high time to try it out for possible specimen bream.

I picked up Colin at seven-thirty yesterday evening and, after spending some time loading the car with four buckets of groundbait which included seven loaves and about 20 lb of dry cereal and all the gear, we were finally on our way.

I had decided beforehand that on arrival at the lake (if the wind permitted — and it did) we would boat fish close to the middle in about twelve feet of water. We heaved the ground bait over the side (marking the area with a float attached to twelve feet of line and a swan shot) and rowed twenty yards away to put down the anchor weights. This was a great mistake: I did not realise that the anchor ropes even when tight would move so much that ledgering was impossible. When either of us moved to recast the boat swayed to and fro, making our ledger bobbins hit the butt ring one minute and drop into the water a second later. There really was nothing we could do so back to the boat house staging we went, having deposited all our groundbait out in the middle. It was pitch dark now and, once we had settled in with our ledger rods firmly placed on the wooden staging, Colin decided to take the car back to his house for some more groundbait.

An hour later he arrived back complete with two buckets of slop to find that, not only had I not had a bite, but that I was nursing a migraine headache. I found it difficult to contemplate continuing fishing and Colin's suggestion of returning to the house before dawn was welcome.

I recovered somewhat after a few hours and we were back at the lake as the mist was clouding from the surface. We rowed out to our pre-groundbaited area to find not a bubble in sight. Most peculiar — we had expected the groundbait to prove irresistable to the bream. We rowed slowly across the lake through the mist looking for bream bubbles and, over on the other side close to a huge bed of lilies hugging the margins, we found them.

Massive clouds were spotting the surface as we eagerly put down the groundbait alongside the lilies and rowed back some ten yards to put up our float rods. The water here was about twelve feet deep and, after about half an hour, crammed full of bream, roach and rudd, all taking our bunches of maggots to size 12 hooks. Strangely, bread was a non-starter; nothing so much as looked at a nice lump of flake. Yet the maggots were sucked in almost immediately they touched the bottom.

From six a.m. until we left at lunchtime they never stopped feeding. In fact, it was boring for we realised that anything in the bream line much above $3^1/_2$ lb was remote. There *were* bigger fish present, but right among the lilies in the shallow water. Every so often a big bronze back would rise out above the pads and crash back in again. I estimated those I saw at 5–7 lb or even larger; but the problems they pose are just too great for the time at my disposal — at least for this season.

Our total catch for the morning weighed over 70 lb and included several rudd bream hybrids, a fish rarely caught in my part of Norfolk. It was nice to watch a float for a change since nearly all my summer fishing these days consists of distance ledgering and watching ledger bobbins.

No wonder there are so many double-figure pike to be had from the lake — the food supply seems never ending. I don't suppose I shall have another bream session this term but, towards November, I shall return for the piking.

It's back to Broadlands again next week. I hope the weather changes quickly, though. It rather seems as though we are entering another period of heatwave conditions. Everyday for the past week has been scorching hot, with the evenings quickly turning chilly and misty. Not good specimen bream weather at all.

G

Tuesday, 17 August

Damp misty night after bright sunshine all day, clear sky.

I visited Broadlands again last night, taking along Andy Jubb who relished the thought of catching a big bream. The weather conditions of late have been really trying. For the last few days it has been extremely hot with not a breath of wind; while at night the temperature drops alarmingly due to the clear sky.

We fished the usual area from eight p.m. until twelve-thirty. Andy had two good bites, and myself, one. They were each very fast — I suspect tench. Whatever the bream were doing they were certainly not feeding.

I shall leave the water well alone now until the weather changes dramatically. I hope for some rain — a rare sight indeed this year — and some windy spells. Then I shall return with more optimism.

Thursday, 19 August

Very damp misty morning followed by strong warm sunlight from seven a.m., no wind.

I took my son Lee along to our group carp water this morning; more to see how low the level had dropped than in the expectation of sport. This continued lack of rain has badly affected our little lake. In swims which held two feet of water six weeks ago bait now rests on the bottom in about ten inches of water. But, as yet, there appears to be no lack of oxygen (thanks to the prolific curly pond weed growth) cr any dead carp. In fact, there were a couple of fish moving along the margins. At first light I had a lightening take from one on a huge lump of flake at the funnel swim but pulled the hook clean when I struck.

Later on, we moved round to the slope swim on the other side of the lake and I rolled a small fish of about 2 lb off the hook. Finally, I managed to hook a baby mirror of 6 oz. At least it made Lee's morning; he is always overjoyed when a fish comes out of the water.

Tuesday, 24 August

*Very damp and misty morning, strong sunshine all day till
dusk, a chilly evening with a clear sky.*

The continued heatwave conditions certainly are frustrating. I am all keyed-
up for seeking those big bream and hate breaking the rhythm, but the cold,
clear nights of late have ruined the chances of returning to Broadlands Lake. I
only hope the weather breaks soon because I would like to have a few more
sessions before switching my attention to zander in mid-September.

Today I was a greedy and fished twice. This morning's session was from
dawn until eight-thirty a.m., and this evening I fished from eight p.m. until
eleven p.m.

Unable to decide whether to go chubbing or to try the carp lake again, I
woke my son Lee up at four a.m. and put on my thinking cap over a cup of
coffee. I finally decided that Lee would not fancy crawling through dew-
soaked grass and nettles after the chub and opted for the group's carp lake.

On arrival, there were a few good fish moving through the surface weed,
but as the mist cleared, so did their movement cease. I did not have a good
run all morning: just short, sharp twitches from the tiny mirrors nibbling at
my lumps of flake. I put up a light rod for Lee with 4 lb line and a size 10
hook covered by a small lump of flake. With this outfit he quickly caught
three little mirrors which we transferred to the stock pond — at least Lee had
enjoyed some sport.

For this evening I had arranged a complete change and, as Nobby Clarke
had requested a roaching trip to the "rushes" stretch of the Wensum a few
days ago, I had fixed up a seven-thirty start. I had not been to the stretch to
see what the conditions were like since my last roaching session there on 22nd
February, so it was with some interest that Nobby and I arrived at the river
after crashing our way through a whole summer's growth of marshland
vegetation. Conditions certainly looked quite promising, with a fair level due
to the mill owner downstream keeping the sluice gates closed and with only a
few patches of cabbages and a little surface weed close in.

The Wensum is always terribly weedy during the summer months but
luckily, because this stretch was dredged two years ago, there is a fair depth
here when the river is full; about eight feet deep in the centre channel where
our baits were to be placed. How different from winter conditions when the
river is being continually run off and kept at a low level of between four and
five feet.

We tackled up with light ledger tackle — 3 lb line with paternosters holding a quarter ounce bomb and a size 8 hook. Not really sporting, perhaps, but if a big roach decides to dive into a bed of cabbages lighter tackle would be quite useless. I scattered out a few free helpings of flake and we settled down to wait for dusk to come, after clipping our isotope bobbins onto the front rod rests.

At this time last year, and well on into September, I took some nice bags of big roach from this very spot on identical tackle and methods. The dace were always first to the bait, nibbling away at a penny-sized lump of flake till one of them could swallow it. Then, as darkness set over the river, a roach shoal would move in. Instead of the ledger bobbin jerking up an inch and then falling back (so typical of dace knocks) it would suddenly go sailing up to the butt ring; and this is what we were waiting for. But the pattern of last year had changed: there were dace skittering about on the surface but our baits were untouched below. Then I had a long positive pull on the bobbin, obviously a roach, but missed it. Nobby had an identical bite several minutes later and also failed to connect. Then we sat there for another two and a half hours till nearly eleven o'clock, without another touch.

An intriguing evening's fishing in that I know the roach were in the swim — perhaps not many — but certainly enough to produce more bites than we had. Then there were the dace — last year at this time they were a positive nuisance. I can only put down this reluctance to feed to the present weather conditions. It appears that within minutes of darkness falling everything stops rolling, moving and eating. I can never remember this happening as much as it has recently.

I think I am going to have another change during this period of inactivity and go chubbing; they always oblige. But I shall certainly try the roach again shortly.

Thursday, 26 August

Chilly misty morning followed by bright hot sunshine, by late afternoon the sky heavily clouded, light breeze.

Today finally saw a change in the weather which, for the fishing I had planned, could not have come at a more opportune moment.

About a week ago Gerry Hughes, assistant editor of the *Anglers Mail* rang to say that he was on holiday in North Norfolk, and what about a roaching session? However, after the terrible conditions of late and the blank roach session the other evening I was in a quandry, so this morning I went along to the Wensum, two miles upstream from the roach stretch, where it narrows and holds numerous chub to see if they were more obliging. If the worst came we could switch over at the last moment for the sake of some sport.

I arrived a little before dawn to find a thick mist hugging the river and walked upstream to where some beds of watercress hung out into the stream, forming rafts. I flipped out a piece of flake and, immediately, a chub of about 2 lb was on. It became heavily weeded during the fight and so the swim was not worth further casts, although generally, if you can extract the first fish fairly quietly, a second is on the cards.

I was more interested in the general state of the river and how it would fish so I meandered further upstream to another swim. Nothing doing at this one, but at the next, a weed raft in the corner of a bend, I netted a nice chub of about $3^1/_2$ lb — again to flake. I hooked this fish at the tail end of the raft and, after releasing it down-stream, I flicked a bait well upstream. An immediate take resulted in the fish bolting downstream towards me and under the raft where it rolled and shed the hook. After losing this one, I carried on walking upstream but failed to tempt any more chub. The river was so weeded from top to bottom that I feared an evening session with Gerry would present too many problems to someone who did not know the river.

I decided to drive down to the rushes to have a look at the river and put some mashed bread in just in case we finally settled on the roach. As it happened, this was a wise move for, around lunchtime, the bright sunshine, which had followed the early morning mist, disappeared. It was replaced by lovely dark clouds. What a beautiful sight after such a long period of scorching days and bitterly cold, misty nights.

When Gerry arrived at the house this evening at seven I told him that we could do a lot worse than switch from chub to roach again as the conditions were so good. He aggreed and, after a cup of coffee, we set off.

At the rushes we set up the ledger tackles with some degree of optimism. The river looked good — oily, but ruffled by crosswinds on the opposite bank. We both fished what I call the end swim, at the downstream part of the fishery, just two yards apart. I put in some mashed bread where out baits would be and we settled down to wait for darkness. I had just told Gerry that the roach would not feed until dark when the bobbin shot up, and in came a nice roach of about $1^1/_2$ lb. In fact it turned out to be a very good night's fishing, compared to recent sessions and a textbook illustration of how the river could fish when on form.

After that first roach, I expected bites at almost anytime from an area downstream of the baited spot. Gerry, however, putting his flake just a few yards upstream of the same area had only a few plucks. The fish were loth to come any further upstream, which was a pity, because I so much wanted him to catch some Wensum roach. I even felt a little guilty at taking a further six fish up to just under 2 lb, before bites ceased. But that's fishing, I suppose. I can recall many occasions when I have been casting within feet of someone having a field day, without so much as a bite myself. We called it a night at about eleven and went back to the house for a bite and some coffee, where we sat chatting till one o'clock in the morning.

A very enjoyable evening and I look forward to Gerry fishing the Wensum again, which he hopes to visit in the winter to sample the long trotting.

Sunday, 29 August

Light SW wind, very overcast from dawn, rain in the air.

Unfortunately, my brother David and I rarely fish together these days as we live over one hundred miles apart. But for this Bank Holiday weekend we had arranged for my family to stay with his until midweek, while he came to Norfolk to fish with me.

At seven a.m. I took Barbara and the children to the station to catch their train for London. As David's train was not due until eleven, I decided to pop along to Taverham pits, which are quite close to the house, to see how Nobby and Maureen Clarke had fared with the bream.

They were concentrating, and had been all night, on a deep, smallish pit called clearwater, baiting with trout pellet paste on paternoster rigs. There had been little activity during the night but Nobby said that about half an hour before I arrived the bream had started to feed. Bites were almost instantaneous after tightening up on the paternoster, with the line sometimes twitching before he had fixed the bobbin on the line.

He could see by the look on my face that I fancied a go, so he gave me a spare rod and I sat next to him while Maureen put the kettle on. The bream were quite difficult to hit. Small twitches sparked off short lifts and then, once the fish had finally nibbled the bait down to swallowing size (small baits produced few bites), the bobbin would fly up to the butt ring.

The area where they were feeding and where Nobby had baited was some fifty yards out, and we missed so many bites. But then I managed to fluke out a couple of 3 lb and 4 lb 9 oz respectively. The time flew by and, at ten o'clock, I left them to meet Dave. I would have liked to stay but Nobby later told me that soon afterwards the feeding spell ended but not before he caught two more, the best going 4 lb 9 oz.

I arrived at the station just as Dave's train came in and, after helping him to load all his gear into the mini, drove home for some lunch and a natter about our tactics for the roach and bream which he was particularly interested in. He fancied going after some good bream to the 5 lb mark and maybe some big roach on the Wensum. I suggested that we have a casual session at the rushes in the afternoon to allow Dave to become familiar with the end swim in its weedy, summer dress, and then a trip to Gunton lake in the evening for the bream.

We took our trotting rods and some maggots along to the rushes and had a very pleasant afternoon. The weather was ideally overcast and the river was running clear and slowly, with piles of newly cut weed floating on top. We did not expect to catch much, so a dozen or so small roach to around 8 oz and a flukey tench of $2^1/_2$ lb on double maggot to a size 16 hook which I caught trotting two feet off bottom (due to the thick weed carpeting the bed) made us happy. The tench was quite a surprise considering that I have ledgered flake during the evening for two summers here and this was the first tench.

After a meal back at the house, we set off at five full of optimism for Gunton. On arrival at the lake we realised that we were not the only optimists around. Most of the swims were occupied by other bream anglers bent on an all-night session. However, we managed to find a vacant clearing in the rushes wide enough for both, fishing two rods apiece.

While Dave unloaded the gear from the car I catapulted a bucket load of groundbait over an area some thirty yards out. We then tackled up, each with a swim feeder and maggots on one rod and paternostered flake on the other.

We had arrived a little too early but darkness soon loomed over the lake accompanied by a rolling mist and a moderate wind off the sea (the lake is only ten miles inland) blowing into our faces. This was strange, because I had telephoned the weather service and had been promised a southerly wind — which would have been on our backs. He also mentioned rain but the conditions looked quite nice, so I discounted it. Well, you can't always believe the meteorologists can you?

At about nine o'clock the wind stopped and we started to get a few twitches on the maggot baits. They were small skimmer bream, which should have been asleep by now, and we caught half a dozen in rapid succession. Then my ledger bobbin moved very slowly but positively up to the butt ring and I hit into one of the better bream which we had come for. It did not fight very much, as some from the lake do, but at a shade over 4 lb it was at least a start. This encouraged Dave who asked what sort of bag we could expect in these conditions. I told him about the catch of twenty-six bream taken by Terry Houseago earlier on in the season. "Right" he said, "I'm going to put my baits out again" and as he said it, I wished I had listened to the weather man. The sky seemed to open as though someone up there had taken the bottom out of a bucket. Within seconds, or so it seemed, a couple of week's rain must have fallen and all the super conditions with their promise of sport to follow just vanished.

We scrambled for the brollies and put our gear under them, becoming drenched in the process. I don't think I had ever before attempted to fish under such a deluge of rain. The thunder crashed all around us and the lightning was so bright that we could see the other anglers scattered around the lake. After an hour sitting there, wet and miserable, only five yards from the tallest oak tree at the lake I suggested that we get the hell out of it. A bolt of lightning zoomed across the trees to our right and Dave agreed.

We piled all the gear into the back of the mini and, feeling like a couple of drowned rats, drove back to the house. What a start to Dave's holiday — the weather always seems to be unkind whenever he journeys to Norfolk to fish with me.

Bank Holiday Monday, 30 August

Very overcast, continual rain from dawn to dusk, sometimes heavy with thunder.

With the disappointment of the previous evening still in our minds, we rose at five-thirty to find that the rain had eased just a little, although it was obviously in for the whole day. I suggested that we might try the Marsh lake which had not been fished by our group since the tench became finicky there in late July. In addition to maggots and groundbait for the swim feeders, we had collected some lobworms which I thought might give us a chance of one of those big perch.

On arrival at the lake I noticed that the blanket weed, so troublesome on my last few visits, had disappeared. Instead, the entire surface was covered in large blotches of green algae, though the water was fairly high and reasonably clear. Nice conditions, in fact.

Dave set up two rods, ledgering worms, and I fished my usual swim feeder rigs to fish maggots on one and brandlings on the other. Almost immediately Dave started to knock out small perch on his lobworms about thirty yards out in eight feet of water. Our decisions to fish the deepest end of the lake had paid off. There appeared to be thousands of small perch in his swim — which was only ten yards to the right of mine — and I could not get a touch by fishing straight out. Changing one bait to a lobworm and keeping maggots on the other, I cast both baits well out to my left. I am not above poaching Dave's fishing but I fancied casting around to different spots in case there were any tench on the prowl.

Within seconds, the indicator on my worm shot up and I was fast into a good fish. I thought at first that I had hooked a tench but that old "eel" feeling ran through the rod and, twisting through the surface, there came an eel of about 2 lb. Fortunately, it spun itself off the hook as I was about to net it. I put another worm out and the very same thing happened — another eel of about 2 lb. Dave wanted this to eat so I despatched it and lowered it into his canvas bucket.

Then, while Dave was merrily knocking out perch to 12 oz I experienced about half-a-dozen tentative bites on the lobworms. The ledger bobbin would rise an inch, drop back, and then zoom up quite fast. All, except one, had started to drop back as I struck but I did eventually connect and with a good fish. I thought, at first, that it was another eel but slowly it started to kite heavily round towards Dave's swim and I knew it was a big tench, played it carefully, not giving it too much stick and, after several heavy runs, it was ready for the net — or so I thought. As Dave was about to slide the net into the water it made one more lunge for which I was not ready. The hook pulled out and I reeled in a slack line.

Angry with myself at losing a fish which was probably well over 5 lb, perhaps even larger, I switched over the other rod to worm and put both baits out into the area where the tench had taken. Alas, there were no more bites except tearaway runs from the little perch. In between the perch we took a couple more goodish eels of between $1^1/_2$ lb and 2 lb, and I tried one of the smaller perch on a paternoster tackle beyond where they were biting in the hope of a big stripey, but to no avail.

We eventually tired of yanking out small perch and took a stroll around the lake to see what was about. Although nothing in the way of big fish was bubbling or moving, at the dam outlet end we came across thousands of small fry, moving about within a foot of the bank in an inch of thick green algae, blown there by the wind. They were far too small to be netted with our landing net but, by quickly lifting algae, mud and fry onto the bank, we found out what they were: baby tench — all between an inch and two inches long. I think, in over twenty-five years of angling, I can only recall catching a handful of tench under a pound in weight and I had never seen shoals of tench fry before. I always assumed that, after hatching, they buried themselves into the bottom weed for protection against predators. Perhaps the general disappearance of weed in the lake at present had made these little fellows find refuge where they could — in an inch of green algae. I certainly hope they find a home before the algae goes because the perch will soon find them.

We left the lake at midday after an enjoyable session, despite the continual rain, and went home for lunch and a rest. For our evening stint we decided to try Gunton lake again for the bream so, armed with another bucket of groundbait, worms, maggots and a loaf, we set off at six p.m. despite the rain. We planned to stay all night if the conditions allowed, but I somehow knew that the weather would deteriorate.

By eleven p.m., after sitting it out in stormy conditions, the wind suddenly changed direction to blow straight in our faces. My brolly promptly bent in half and flew out of the ground, to crash into the trees behind me. This got a laugh out of Dave who agreed that to continue fishing was a waste of time, not that sport had been brisk, anyway. We had taken one bream apiece of about $4^1/_2$ lb each and missed just a few bites. Dave's fish came to lobworms and mine to maggots. It seems that shallow lake bream do not like heavy rain. Perhaps the continual drumming sound close above their heads makes them disinclined to move because there certainly appeared to be few fish over the groundbait.

Wet through again, we were back at the house at midnight and glad to be there.

Tuesday, 31 August

Rain at first, brighter later without a cloud in the sky.

Todays conditions made a welcome change from the past two days and the lack of rain made me think that a trip to Broadlands lake after the bream would really make David's holiday, especially if he connected with a seven pounder. I was a little worried, however, that the sky was too clear and that it would become colder after dark. But Dave was keen to visit the lake and at six-thirty we set off to be ready to fish by dusk.

The boats were out of commission, being half filled with water, so we chose to fish from the staging close to the area where I usually take the bream. We catapulted a big helping of groundbait out and set up two rods apiece with paternostered flake on each. Immediately on David's left was a huge patch of lilies and I suggested that, if the bream were off, he might flick a bait close to them to see if the tench were about. He put in a few balls of groundbait over the lilies, as insurance, and we sat back to await events.

During the first hour of darkness there was a lot of activity. Bream were bow-waving across the surface and roach in their hundreds were boiling on top, but bites were slow. I had three good bream bites, taking the bobbin slowly up to the butt ring, and I missed them all. Then I caught a small roach of around six ounces and after that all went dead. There was nothing moving near the groundbait due, I think, to the temperature dropping quite suddenly. I felt a little chilly as I always do when sport is slow but Dave had little time to feel cold. He had put a lump of flake out close to the lilies, after having absolutely nothing at distance over the groundbait, and immediately caught a good tench. It was a long female — badly out of condition though, even in its thin state, it weighed 4 lb 11 oz — beating David's best-ever tench by an ounce. A few minutes later he had another of 4 lb 3 oz, which was nearly lost around the supports of the staging. Hitting into them at such short range means that they have a little left for last-minute dives, and I warned him of this. He put in a few more balls of groundbait around the lilies and, within minutes, had another bite which he missed. Then he took another tench — a male of 3 lb 14 oz — and missed another two bites before all activity ceased about midnight.

It is most peculiar how these shallow-lake tench are prepared to feed in low air temperatures, whilst the bream are not. I have noticed this several times this summer and cannot think why a fish which, for most of the year is the freshwater fish most susceptible to low temperatures, goes rampantly on the feed during the coldest part of a summer's night when everything else is uninterested.

I was glad that Dave had enjoyed some good sport, though I would still like him to catch a big bream. Our wives are returning tomorrow so I suppose our evening sessions will have to stop, but we shall sneak a roaching session later on in the week at the rushes.

Friday, 3 September

Overcast all day and into the evening with a light northerly wind, sky cleared to show a bright moon from nine p.m.

As we had not been roaching this week, Dave and I tried the rushes on the Wensum last night accompanied by my son Lee who had been pestering us to go fishing.

When we started at seven p.m. the conditions — an overcast sky and a full, slow river, without weed floating on top — were excellent. We put in a little mashed bread downstream of the "end" swim and ledgered flake over it, sitting just two yards apart. As darkness came, the roach started feeding and, after cursing myself for missing several good bites, I connected with a heavy roach which immediately started to storm off downstream. It felt quite large (certainly over 2 lb) and, as I slowly gained line to pump it upstream, the hook fell out quite suddenly. The hook seemed all right, but I changed it, anyway, and recast.

Dave was having trouble casting accurately at first and often overcast, to land his bait in the marginal weeds on the other bank. But he found the clear run after a while and started to get some bites. Then, suddenly, the river started to flow quite strongly and we became hampered by floating weed. We pinched some swan shot onto the bobbin lines to counteract the flow and, although this held against the flow, whenever a clump of weed hit the line the bobbin shot up just like a bite.

Dave complained that all this week we have been beaten by conditions and I commiserated with him, for there was really nothing to do but hit every bite, even though ninety per cent of them were really weed clumps.

Shortly after, the river started to pull caused, I presume, by the mill owner downriver opening his sluice gates to let some of the recent rain water through. The clouds vanished and out came a bright moon accompanied by mist patches. It was not exactly encouraging but we felt certain that the roach were still feeding because, every so often, one would roll heavily in the swim. This became quite apparent when I casually hit into another weed bite which hit back: a roach of about $1\frac{1}{2}$ lb.

This encouraged Dave, who was about to call it a night, and we both started to concentrate more. When, a little later, there appeared to be less weed coming down to foul our lines we were quite optimistic. In fact, we were so optimistic, now that bites were plainly visible (although we could not connect) that I took Lee home at midnight, cold and tired, to return for some more action. But it was not to be. We fished through, despite the cold, to nearly two a.m., having the occasional half hearted bite but missing them all.

An interesting but irritating session. It looks as though David will have to wait until his next visit, probably in a few months time, to catch that two-pound roach.

AFTERTHOUGHT

I have been wondering why we missed so many roach bites yesterday evening and am certain that our striking was at fault. Instead of striking up and to our right against the flow we should have struck low and to our left, directly away from the swim because, due to the strong flow, a tremendous bow in the line is created when fishing with bobin indicators. Or we could have fished a tight line and watched our rod tips.

I must remember this for future occasions for I am sure that, had I realised this yesterday evening, we would have taken several fish. We were simply not straightening the line out on the strike. I could kick myself.

Wednesday, 8 September

Light westerly wind, sky very overcast, hint of rain, warm.

In today's weather conditions, the prospect of accounting for some big roach on the Wensum at the "Rushes" look excellent. However, for some inexplicable reason, Steve Harper and I fished there this evening in the "end" swim from seven until eleven with little to show for our efforts.

I hinted to Steve, as darkness loomed over the river with the moon hazed over by drifting clouds, that we could be in for a good catch. For half an hour, in which a couple of bites materialized to our ledgered flake, I would have put money on it. There appeared to be some fish in the swim, though, curiously, none were rolling as they do here after dark, and I very soon connected with a roach-bream of about $1^{1}/_{4}$ lb. It had a couple of deep cuts near the tail, an obvious pike attack, which could very well have happened while I was playing it — for a second or two there was stalemate, as though the fish had become weeded and then, suddenly, it was free again.

After this, we fished on thinking that, any minute, the roach would come on and with the occasional twitch (gudgeon possibly), but it was not to be.

I wonder if a pike was lying in the swim making the roach reluctant to move to our baits, or if the still. windless conditions were not conducive to sport. I did not see a roach roll all evening long either up or downstream, and yet, previously I had seen at least a couple of good roach swirl on the surface immediately after dark on every evening I have fished this part of the Wensum. It is almost a ritual with Wensum roach. A disappointing session.

Friday, 10 September

Light westerly wind, overcast, rain in the air.

I had not intended to go fishing this evening, but the conditions looked so good for a spot of roaching at the rushes that, by seven o'clock, I could stand it no longer. Within five minutes, I had gathered the gear together and accompanied by Lee, who is becoming really keen despite the blanks of late, we set off for the "end" swim on the Wensum.

Again the river looked good, but not a single roach rolled as darkness set in. We sat there for two hours without a twitch to the ledgered flake — most odd. The river appears dead and I cannot think of a reason for the inactivity, particularly as the present weather conditions are, in my experience of the Wensum, practically perfection. It just goes to show how wrong you can be, and how misleading weather conditions can be.

We arrived home at half past nine, but did not relax for very long because, a few minutes later, there was a knock on the front door and in burst Maureen Clarke, bubbling over with excitement. She and Nobby had been roaching on the Wensum, near Drayton, at a spot we call "dead bodies", and Nobby had just landed a huge roach on ledgered breadflake. His scales were not working and Maureen asked if I would bring my set down for a weigh-in, which I was only too pleased to do. I followed Maureen's car down to the river where we found Nobby concentrating hard on his isotope bobbin. All had been quiet since Maureen's departure to fetch me so he reeled in his tackle and crept upstream along the bank to fetch the keepnet holding the big roach.

Inside was one of the nicest roach I think I have ever seen: quite a short fish but deep and thick set. I guessed it to be around 2 lb 6 oz but, when hoisted on to my set of Avons in the weigh net, it surprised us all by scaling 2 lb 11 oz. A superb fish, so immensely thick around the middle, and, of course, Nobby was ecstatic.

We took several photographs and immediately afterwards Nobby returned it to the water. We then crept back to his swim to see if he could tempt any

Nobby Clark with a fine roach

more and, although he had two tentative bites (both missed), he just could not concentrate. He stared down at the isotope and kept repeating to himself — "2 lb 11 oz — blimey! — 2 lb 11 oz".

I left Maureen and a very happy Nobby at the river and made tracks through the wood towards the car. It was very nice, as it always is, to share in a friend's joy when he has finally achieved a lifelong ambition: and Nobby's roach was certainly that.

Sunday, 12 September

Westerly wind with heavy morning rain, followed by overcast but dry conditions for remainder of the day.

I returned at lunchtime from my first zander trip of the season to the Great Ouse Relief Channel at Downham Market. It was the sort of morning where, had we been able to stay on almost anything could have happened.

Certainly the zander were still active and taking deadbaits, and might have carried on feeding in the cloudy conditions all day, but because they are such an unpredictable species, living in one of the most unpredictable and moody waters I fish, one can never be sure.

The morning started very slowly indeed and, after sitting out a thunder storm from dawn till around seven-thirty a.m. (usually the most active period for zander), Terry Houseago and I wondered if we would have any runs at all. Then, after the torrential rain had stopped, a thick mist rolled along the channel making for better conditions. Almost within minutes of the mist forming, Terry had a long positive run to a dead roach, ledgered on the bottom some thirty yards out and, on striking, connected with a good fish which immediately started to take line. He played it carefully for several minutes, during which time it surfaced close in; it looked to be around the 10 lb mark but we could not tell whether it was a zander or a pike due to the thick water colour. We still do not know for, seconds later, Terry's line went slack and he reeled in a badly frayed 8 lb line.

Unfortunately, losing fish on the Relief Channel is a common occurence due to clumps of blue-black zebra mussels. These razor-sharp molluscs live in huge colonies along the steep ledges close to the margins and almost anywhere along the bottom. We have both lost so many fish due to our lines being frayed by zebras that we accept it philosophically. Strangely, I cannot ever remember coming across these mussels on any other water, only on the Relief Channel.

Very soon Terry was in again, but a smaller fish this time and by the way it was fighting, a certain pike; and so it proved — a seven-pounder. Then his other rod was away and in came our first zander of the season, a baby of 2 lb on a 5-inch dead roach.

Things were certainly looking up as the mist started slowly to disappear showing heavy clouds high up in the sky, with a bright haze — breaking through every so often. My own rods became active but I completely missed a scorching twenty-yard run on a small dead roach and within minutes, snapped on a dace of the same size on the strike. On reeling in I found the line was frayed — zebras again!

Of course, many of these bust ups would be avoided if we float-fished the baits instead of ledgering them on the bottom, but past experience has shown that the freshly-killed static deadbait, punctured with a knife to let out some of the aroma before casting, outfishes livebaits off the bottom by a mile — at least as far as zander are concerned.

We use a particularly effective method of bite detection when ledgering dead baits, in conjunction with a running paternoster and a one ounce arlesy bomb for distance. After casting, the rod is placed in the rest — carp fashion — pointing at the bait and, from an open bale arm, a loop of line is lightly nipped through an elastic band already positioned on the rod handle opposite the spool. We then fold a two-inch square of silver kitchen foil over the line a few inches in front of the rod tip. With several rods spaced out along the bank at ten-yard intervals, to locate the zander shoals, we can easily see from a central point the slightest twitch or run to any of the baits. A classic run is when the silver foil flies away from the rod down into the water as the line pops out of the rubber band and flows from the spool. Not all runs are like this: sometimes just a yard of line goes and then the bait is ejected, usually by immature zander or eels. It is an interesting way of ledgering a deadbait because the silver foil acts as a float and helps to sustain one's interest during the long periods of inactivity.

But to return to this mornings zandering: a lull occurred after my missed runs and we waited until nearly ten o'clock with just a few half-hearted, two-feet pulls on a couple of the baits. Little zander with big ideas. Then, all of a sudden, one of my small baits, a gudgeon, was away and I quickly closed the

Zebra mussels and gudgeon bait

H

bale for a quick strike before it dropped it. Everything held and I brought in a scrappy zander of $4^1/_4$ lb. Not big by any means, but a start. No sooner had I unhooked it and dropped it into the big keep net than my other rod was away — gudgeon again. For a moment I felt a goodish fish pulling on the other end and then all went slack.

Yes — zebras again — blasted things!

I retackled and whipped out another gudgeon which was savagely taken within seconds of hitting the bottom, just as I was opening the bale arm to secure a loop of line. Missed it, though.

About ten minutes passed, after casting yet again and then the same rod was off on a scorching run which promptly came to an abrupt end as I struck: another frayed line, thanks to the zebras. I retackled and had to wait but two or three minutes for another run. Luckily this time, all held and another zander was on; another scrappy fish larger than the first at 5 lb but thumping the rod tip heavily from hooking to netting. They really are an active fish when hooked, similar to how one would imagine a huge perch would fight — dogged resistance all the way.

Terry moved one of his rods into the "taking" area and we both had several runs, all missed, before we had to make for home at eleven.

Hunting zander in the Relief Channel, a yearly pilgrimage for me from now until early November when the frosts cut their activity down, is always a chancy business. Being eleven miles long by over one hundred yards wide with an average depth in the centre of around fourteen feet, makes it a formidable water, so this was a satisfying session.

Tuesday, 14 September

Very overcast, light northerly wind, cool.

I tried again for the roach this evening with some measure of success, but the Wensum along at the Rushes is still in a dour mood.

I started, as usual, a little before dark by putting in a handful of mashed bread and paternostered a lump of flake over it. Again there were no roach rolling but, as darkness fell, I had two bites and hit both — roach of 1 lb and $1^1/_4$ lb, respectively.

I expected more to follow in the three hours I sat there staring at the isotope bobbin but, apart from weed bites (there is still a fair amount floating down), not another twitch did I have in apparently good conditions from a part of the river really prolific in fish. Most curious.

Thursday, 16 September

Very overcast, moderate northerly wind, rain at times, intermittent sunshine in afternoon.

After last Sunday's zander trip to the Relief Channel I was keen to return for some more action so I took the day off. In the company of Sid Johnson and his father, we left Norwich at four a.m. in order to start fishing on the Channel at Downham Market by dawn.

Being very overcast and windy, the conditions were terrific for some zander action but the dawn period, usually the most hectic; did not produce it. My first run came at half past seven — a positive, long run to a small gudgeon paternostered some sixty yards out, resulting in a fish of about 5 lb. Within minutes of putting another gudgeon out to the same area I hooked into a better fish which fought hard and doggedly all the way to the net. It was short and fat and pulled the spring balance down to 7 lb 10 oz, equalling my previous best from the water caught last year.

It was not a bad start, but they were very localised and not roaming along the middle of the Channel where one expects a run on almost any of the rods. There appeared to be a small group of zander about two thirds of the way across opposite one rod. They were not roaming, in fact, they seemed to have moved further out which was proved by an instant run when I changed my ounce bomb over to one of two ounces for greater distance. I missed this and also another run a few minutes later, although I pricked the second fish momentarily. The rods on either side of me remained inactive for the entire session.

After the initial runs which stopped at about ten a.m., there appeared to be very little activity except for some large roach rolling quite close to the bank on the drop off, where the marginal water of two feet suddenly falls down to over twelve feet.

At noon, when it seemed that there would be no more zander, I had two tentative runs in quick succession, the second of which I hit, which resulted in a small zander of about 3 lb. Then there was a long lull during which we discussed what time we should depart and settled for two o'clock. I agreed for sport seemed dead, even though some sunny spells had broken through the

The author with a 9lbs 3½oz zander

clouds to give alternating light values which often spur zander into a feeding mood.

At a few minutes to two, my silver foil indicator flew from the rod about two yards down towards the water and then stoppped. I looked at the line which was not pulling from the spool and then at a nearby swan, swimming away from the spot where my line entered the water. Apparently it was a line bite but, as I started to reel in, I changed my mind. There was a slight jiggling feeling on the line to which I responded by a quick, hard strike. Immediately, a heavy fish started to take line close to the bottom in fifteen feet of water. I was taken aback and delighted all at once and started to enjoy a fight from what was obviously a big zander. I pumped it most of the way in close to the drop off, where it repeatedly dived to the bottom and I could feel my ledger

116

bomb grating on the shelf of zebra mussels. Luckily, the paternoster did not foul and, after quite a tussle, I brought the fish to the surface where Sid was ready with the net.

Being some fifteen feet higher than the water and three yards back on the flood bank, I could not stop it from coming close into the bank where it became jammed in the marginal weed. As I tried to bully it towards the net the hooks fell out. Sid reacted very smartly, thank goodness, and whipped the net under it before it righted itself and swam off. We quickly heaved it up to the bank and straight onto the scales which showed 9 lb $3^1/_2$ oz. It was my best zander to date — and a particularly deep-bodied, clean-looking fish.

It had been worth hanging on after all and we stayed another hour in case of further activity, which did not come. At three o'clock we packed up all the gear and made the long walk back to the car.

A terrific day's sport for me, but I was sorry that Sid and his Dad, who has never caught a zander, could not share in my jubilation; but there are many more trips to come.

Saturday, 17 September

Very misty, damp morning, still misty at nine a.m.

I decided this morning to have a few hours chubbing on the Wensum at Drayton before work.

This part of the Wensum used to be a chubber's paradise — not too wide, with alder and willow trees overhanging the bankside providing numerous raft-type swims where the summer weed gathered around branches lapping the surface. In fact, the entire $^3/_4$-mile stretch was really one big chub swim with anything from half a dozen to twenty chub lying beneath each raft.

However, since my visit here last Autumn, the land owners have obviously done a clearing job on the bankside vegetation to reclaim more grazing land for their cattle. In the process they have taken half the chub swims away. I was quite shocked when I saw the stretch at first light, I thought for a moment that I was on a different river. Without trees and bushes the Wensum here looks almost like a canal.

Nevertheless, I followed the river downstream past the park-like bankside, until I found three favourite old swims where alders overhang the far bank and concentrated on these. My freelined lobworm on size 4 hook was grabbed within seconds of landing close to the first raft and, as the line tightened quickly through the water, I hit hard. Back across the river flew the hook. When I crept quietly downstream a few yards to put a bait at the rail end of the raft the very same thing happened again, the hook just pricking and, obviously, spooking the fish for no more bites came from that swim.

At the second raft my big lobs were again taken with confidence and I took a chub of 3 lb 6 oz on the first cast — a long fish, very lean in the belly, but fighting well in the still, weedy water. I pricked another one on the second cast and then lost a goodish fish just when I was getting the better of it. Then bites ceased. The third raft produced absolutely nothing and, by this time, I had overstayed my two hours so I trudged back to the car and went off to work.

A pleasant outing, despite my missing out on at least four chub.

Thursday, 23 September

Thin drizzle and very overcast from dawn till nine a.m. then very warm and sunny, slight southerly wind.

After the excellent zander sport of late, I decided to take today off and, with Andy Jubb who had not been zandering since last October when we took a good bag of some eleven fish, visited the Relief Channel at Downham Market.

We were at our favourite location a little before dawn, armed with plenty of small baits in case the zander were feeding well as the conditions indicated. We had to wait a good hour into daylight before the first runs started. They were all to my rods and I missed six scorching takes to paternostered gudgeon before I finally made contact with the culprits. They were small zander of about 2 lb apiece and seemed to be very thick on the ground.

As usual I concentrated my baits well over to the far side of the Channel whilst Andy covered the middle and near water. His baits remained untouched but mine were constantly being grabbed by little zander. I ended up with five and one eel of about a pound. I suppose some of the runs I missed could have been from good fish, but I rather fancied that only small zander were in the area, which was rather disappointing.

The Relief Channel is a vast drain with massive shoals of various sized zander. Sometimes big fish are found in with the smaller ones, sometimes not. It is as simple as that. Although I always put out larger baits when troubled by small zander, today they remained untouched but when I changed over to gudgeon again a 2 lb zander grabbed hold.

Even the little zander became uninterested around noon and, just in case the larger fish moved into the area, we stayed another two hours, but without another run. At two p.m. we decided to call it a day, at least as far as the zander were concerned, and visit the river Wissey, only a fifteen-minute drive from the Relief Channel, for some chub.

The river Wissey, near Stoke Ferry, is such an excellent chub river I always take along some lobworms when zandering on the channel in case of poor sport. As it is some forty miles from home I rarely have the opportunity of fishing it — most of my chubbing sessions tend to be two-hour sessions before work.

We stopped in the village for a loaf of bread and arrived a little while later on the banks of what used to be an intimate little river, clean flowing over beds of gravel, with nicely overgrown banks. But it was no longer the river

A Specimen Fishing Year

where only last year I had stalked and caught some good chub. Obviously,
since last year, a dredger had been active, tearing away at the bankside
shrubbery and piling it in neat high mounds on both banks. I don't know how
the River Authority have the gall to call such sacrilege "river maintenance".
The lush beds of streamer weed were gone, as were the alder bushes and the
sandy bars where big roach and dace could be seen. As for chub, usually
easily seen here even on a cloudy day, there were none.

We walked about a mile upstream following the dredger's path and came
upon a small cabin cruiser tied up in a layby cut back into the bank where a
willow once hung over the river — a superb chub swim. Could these madmen
be widening, deepening and ruining this beautiful little river for navigation?

We walked on further than I had ever fished before and, eventually
reached a spinney on our own bank beyond which the dredger had not gone.
The Wissey, as I knew it, at last. Andy chose a bend at the downstream end of
the spinney and I walked above it to where a small dyke joined the main
stream.

I put in some floating crusts just above the dyke and settled in amongst the
nettles to see what happened. On previous occasions the Wissey chub have
been suckers for floating crust and soon I saw that they had not altered their
feeding habits, even if their river had been ruined downstream. As the first
crust floated by the mouth of the dyke there was a bow wave and then a huge
boil, followed immediately afterwards by another and another till all the
crusts had disappeared.

The very next crust contained my hook and was quickly taken by a fish of
perhaps $2^1/_2$ lb. The next weighed a shade less and the last, about $3^1/_2$ lb. The
shoal had moved way downstream by now, as chub do when on the crusts and
being caught, and my line was sinking too much for me to float a crust down,
so I walked down towards Andy's swim to see if I could interest another shoal
with the intention of returning to the "dyke" swim later on.

As I was walking merrily along, warmed by the action so far and looking
through the polaroids for more fish, there came a loud voice behind me
saying, "Who the hell are you?" It was an irate farmer who, in no uncertain
terms, told me to clear off.

I tried to pacify him with the Wilson charm but he was not having any and
so Andy and I reluctantly left this upstream haven and returned below the
spinney to the dredged part. Andy was as upset as me. He had taken one chub
and was keyed up for more when I gave him the bad news.

We tried the dredged part for about an hour on a slow bend where our
worms were taken by some eels and a small perch. But our hearts were not in

120

fishing this dead piece of water. The dredger's work had slowed the Wissey's flow almost to a standstill, so floating crusts were out. It is ironic that a machine bent on helping the flow of a river can actually kill it. Dredgers ought to be banned on non-navigable upper rivers. They wreck the anglers sport for many years in addition to turning a charming little river into a featureless drain.

We left for home at half past four feeling frustrated.

Wednesday, 29 September

Cloudy, mild, hint of rain.

I went along to the Wensum, at Ringland, this morning for an hour and a half's chubbing before work. I had plenty of worms collected from the lawn last night and wandered along, freelining them down the streamy runs and under the undercut banks. This particular part of the river is lacking in bankside trees and shrubs, making for very few obvious chub swims. Fishing "blind" is rather tedious — you have to bash away at every likely-looking glide, knowing full well that there may not be a chub within a hundred yards.

Nevertheless, I did pick up one, a three pounder, on the inside of a deep bend and, a little later, a dace of about 6 oz which greedily gobbled up my No. 4 hook holding a huge lob. These were my only bites of the session.

I found several nice roachy-looking glides, however — long, deepish swims — which are bound to hold big roach and I have made a note of them for winter fishing.

Thursday, 30 September

Heavy rain at first light followed by intermittent spells of cloud and bright sunlight for remainder of the day, mild.

I was lucky enough to be able to arrange another zander session for today whilst a friend looked after the shop. I like these all-day sessions in midweek because the Relief Channel is deserted and the spot I like to fish is always vacant.

Maureen and Nobby Clark, both looking forward to their first crack at zander, were at the house by four a.m. and we speedily made our way to the

Channel, picking up Terry Houseago en route.

We commenced fishing a little before first light and, within seconds of putting out the small deadbaits, I was fast into a brace of medium-size zander, one on a gudgeon and the other on a dace, both about 4 lb. Then there was a short lull until just after daybreak followed by the most hectic feeding spell I have ever encountered on the Channel. All came to my rods on the small, slit deadbaits. I had run after run — missing a few, then landing a fish, missing a few more, snapping up on zebra's and then landing another, and so on.

This run of bites was remarkable for the others rods were only a few yards from me yet the zander shoal, and there must have been close on a hundred,

A fine zander catch

was in a very small area. It was a mini hot spot within my usual swim which I consider almost a hot spot in itself. Terry was constantly clambering down the slippery banks to net my fish, and jokingly, moaning at his lack of runs. In about one and a half hours I had at least twenty-five runs of assorted types while Terry's rods, just five yards away, remained inactive despite us using identical tackle and casting the same distance — some seventy yards out.

Up to eight a.m., his only fish was caught on one of my rods while I was playing another. This brought the total bag to nine zander varying from 4 lb to 6 lb 11 oz. Then Terry took one of 5 lb 5 oz on his own gear, at last, and shortly afterwards the feeding-spell ended.

Meanwhile, Maureen had taken a pike of $5\frac{1}{2}$ lb and missed a couple of runs, and Nobby had landed one zander of $2\frac{1}{2}$ lb. It was his first and that, at least, made him happy. After all this excitement we fished on till about three in the afternoon with just one more short burst of action when three of our lines all shot out at once. This was immediately after some heavy cloud had allowed bright sunshine to break through which often spurs zander into action. The runs were missed, though.

We talked on the way home about the day's events, and how finicky zander can be. During the mad feeding spell lots of half-hearted runs occurred. The line would quickly tighten through the water as a fish grabbed the bait but then fall back, just as fast, as though some resistance (the elastic band, I suppose) had deterred the fish.

There is no way of avoiding these tentative runs; we need lead to reach the fish and we need to have a way of retaining the reel line until a run occurs. Leaving a lot of slack line out only invites trouble with zebras as it trails along the bottom. I wish I could think of a way of giving line more sensitively at the slightest hint of a zander run because I am certain that some of these dropped bites are from good fish.

Next time I visit the Channel I shall have both my rods pointing at the baits within two feet of where I sit, instead of placing them ten yards apart. I can then release the line from the rubber bands as soon as the line tightens.

Even with a tight line I managed to snap up on no less than four fish today — thanks to zebras. The line parted gently as I struck and, on reeling in, the line was ripped to shreds.

I also lost a big fish which I hooked on a particularly long cast. It came towards me, kiting to my left from the moment I struck and, after about forty seconds of pumping like mad to raise it off the bottom, the hooks pulled free. After putting in so many sessions on the Channel during the past three seasons this is only the second large fish I have ever hooked. I also snapped up on the first one — I think both were big pike.

A thoroughly enjoyable day, as fishing in the company of Maureen, Nobby and Terry always is.

Thursday, 7 October

Rain at first light, gale force SW winds all day.

Today was one of those days when the weather spoiled the potentially excellent zander conditions of a high and coloured Relief Channel. The gale force south-westerly winds lashed downstream and across the channel into our faces making casting difficult and erecting an umbrella impossible.

David Walls and I arrived at my usual spot as the day was breaking, to find Terry Houseago already fishing with a small zander of about $1^1/_2$ lb in the net — his first run. We hurriedly cast our small deadbaits as far as the wind would allow (about fifty yards instead of seventy) and sat back to wait for the usual hectic dawn feeding spell, which never came. David connected with his only run of the day at about eight o'clock — a zander of exactly five pounds. Terry took an eel of 2 lb 5 oz an hour later and an hour before we packed up at lunchtime, I managed to connect with my only run of the morning, a zander of $5^1/_2$ lb. At least we had not blanked. The session was particularly frustrating because I felt certain that, if the wind had not been so strong and we had been able to reach the usual area with our baits, we would have taken some good fish in the excellent water conditions.

By lunchtime, the wind had increased to make it impossible to continue fishing. Even a two-ounce bomb cast directly across the channel was blown back, eventually to settle just thirty yards from the bank. David and I, reluctantly and frustratedly, left the Channel and drove back to Norwich for a crack at some roach fishing on the Upper Yare, at Trowse.

With the relief channel being so high and coloured I imagined, especially with all the rain of late, that the Yare would fish well, but after an hour's trotting in crystal clear water, with the summers weed still irritatingly sprouting up from the bottom and with the wind blowing gustily down the river, we packed up yet again to try elsewhere.

We settled for Earsham on the Upper Waveney, near Bungay. It's the spot I always go to when all else fails and all we wanted was some reasonably easy fishing after a morning on the windswept Channel. Although the river was lacking in colour there was a reasonably good flow and, from around three

Terry Houseago holding a channel eel

p.m. until dark we managed to extract a couple of dozen roach to just over the pound mark, on maggots. I enjoyed using my trotting rod seriously other than using it to take zander baits and thoughts of big roach crossed my mind all afternoon. I hope the Wensum colours up early this winter, so I can visit the "Rushes" very soon.

I looked at the stretch a few days ago, and apart from the river still running quite clear — the summer weed along the bottom was still evident. I think a few frosts are in order to put the river in good trotting trim.

Thursday, 14 October

Strong, variable South to South Easterly winds accompanied by long periods of rain, sometimes heavy.

In today's nasty weather, Doug Allen and I could not really have picked a better water to start our winter's piking than "the Conifers" Lake, though, the lake being completely surrounded by tall trees, the wind, which came in gusts from different directions made presentation of the static herring very difficult. One minute our floats were being dragged quickly along to either side of the boat and the next blown in towards us.

Our position, in about ten feet of water where most of our pike on previous trips have come, was a mistake really and, after absolutely nothing from our dawn start at seven a.m. to around eleven, we decided to move back towards the boathouse where a part of the lakes surface was evenly ruffled and not affected by crosswinds. We should have moved earlier but torrential rain prevented it.

After putting down no less than four anchor weights to keep the boat steady the action started. Our rods, all fishing herrings well over depth on sliding floats, were spread nicely in a wide arc, some close in to the boat and some far out. It was Doug's float, nearest to the boat, which went first. It was not an electrifying run as many are from this particular lake, just a small "bob" and then a slow glide away. Doug set the hooks firmly while I cleared the other rods.

Judging by the full curve of Doug's rod it was a good pike, obviously high into double figures and fighting fiercely, as do all these Conifers pike. They are exceptional fish as far as fighting capabilities are concerned, and make Broads pike seem positively senile. After a few minutes, Doug seemed to have the better of it, although it was staying deep and coming in quickly towards

126

the boat; too quickly, in fact and, despite Doug putting on full pressure, the fish shot right under the boat and promptly wrapped the trace around one of the anchor ropes. I quickly raised the anchor but the trace was broken. We were both disappointed after waiting five hours for one of the floats to move and then to lose the fish.

After about half an hour one of my floats shot off and I made contact with a ten-pounder. This too fought surprisingly strongly for its size and, no sooner had I unhooked and returned it, than my other float was away. Another good fight and a fish of similar size to the first.

We then had a long period of inactivity during which time I could feel a migraine headache coming on. The non-stop downpour of rain did not help and, within a short time, I could not have cared less about the fishing. At one time I even dreaded getting a run as my head could not have taken the strain. What did I get? Yes, a run, and a good one which I feebly hit into while Doug started to clear the other rods. Unfortunately, this particular pike shot towards the boat like a rocket and, with two of the other lines still out, immediately became tangled. We were in a pickle! Me, with my headache, holding onto a pike which slowly went round the boat three times, and Doug also turning in circles trying to unravel the mess of lines and floats.

They don't make them like they used to!

Eventually, to the accompaniment of much cursing, I netted a long lean fish of about 14 lb (I could not summon up enough energy to weigh it) and we sat down once more. After we had sorted out the tangles I stood up to make a cast and another catastrophe happened. I had just said to Doug that I was going to make one of my special casts (hinting that I could cast further than him) and there was a loud crack as I bent the rod into the wind! I was left holding a short butt and a splintered — 4 piece rod. The bottom joint of my tench-tamer (I use these rods for everything) had snapped in three places. It was either laugh or cry, so we laughed. It must have done me good because after a while I realised that my headache had practically gone.

About an hour before dusk one of my floats suddenly made off. I hit it immediately and a really good fish started to rip line from the reel. It slogged away down deep for a few minutes, but eventually tired and I pumped it towards the boat. I was congratulating myself on a nice fish of sixteen pounds or larger, but we did not find out. About two yards from the net it suddenly dived and, like Doug's fish, ran right under the boat. My rod tip was pulled under the water as I hung on with a tight line so it could not foul the anchor rope, it did, though, and I reeled in a frayed line.

On the way home we chatted about the day's unusual events — especially since neither of us had ever before lost a pike under the anchor rope. It was just one of those days.

Sunday, 17 October

Slight ground frost with mist at dawn, strong sunlight later accompanied by a light southerly wind.

Doug Allen and I fancied a bit of long trotting this morning at the Rushes on the Wensum.

The river looked in good trim when we tackled up in the half light of dawn. Doug chose his favourite bush swim while I tried the end swim. There was a good flow and most of the summer streamer weed had gone, leaving just the odd dying cabbage patch and dark green silk weed on the bottom. A few good frosts will soon kill this off.

After trotting my swim for almost an hour without a bite and with nothing rolling on top, as Wensum roach do if mist coincides with dawn, I walked up to Doug's swim. He was biteless, too, so I took a walk further upstream to catapult some maggots into the top glide to see if anything was moving.

Again no sign of a fish but, after a few trots down, I heard a heavy swirl way upstream in quite shallow water — not a part of the river I often fish. A few seconds later there was another swirl and I saw a large dorsal fin as the fish went down. Off I walked again and settled in opposite the roach activity. I put some maggots in, followed down with the float and got an instant bite which I missed. The second was also missed but I hit into the third and a good roach thumped away on the other end. I played it carefully, thinking it was much larger than it turned out to be — 1 lb 10 oz. I hit into a larger one on the next cast and it started to run steadily upstream when the hook fell out. The next cast produced one of about a pound which shook itself off as I was about to net it and then the swim went dead; swirls on the top had stopped and strong sunlight glared down upon the river. I could see how clear it was and decided to walk back down to Doug.

He had had but one bite, rolled the fish, and no more. I trudged back to the end swim where I had started the morning and where I had left a few livebaits and my pike rod just in case the roach were unco-operative. It was as well I did because the end swim was alive with pike, all small between four and six pounds — nuisance fish to the keen roach man. I caught two — putting them in a dyke full of dace which runs behind the river and missed another four. I think the baits were too big or it was the same pike which could not learn, or a mixture of both.

I think I shall have to plan a pike — only session on the river to extract a few from the best roach swims. I don't mind the odd big one — indeed I welcome them, for their feeding spells are less common than jacks which can easily ruin a mornings roaching by their repeated attacks on hooked fish.

Monday, 18 October

Steve Harper came into the shop at lunchtime today to bring the news of a big pike he had caught from the Bure, near Wroxham, yesterday morning. It weighed 25 lb 11 oz and is a new record for our Broadland Specimen Group. The fish, which was 43 inches long and in prime condition, accepted a livebait being trailed behind the boat.

Well done Steve!

I

Thursday, 21 October

Southerly wind sometimes strong, showers for most of the day.

I sit writing this with an aching back brought about by sitting from dawn until dusk in a boat which was bobbing about for most of the time. But the fishing was worth it.

Doug Allen, Dave Wall, Martin Page and I visited a large, very deep broad near Horning — a new water for our piking exploits although Doug and Dave had fished it for bream several years back. Eager to find out the piking potential, and armed with a good supply of fresh herrings and a few livebaits, we rowed away from the moorings at first light making for the deep water at the far end of the Broad.

Martin and I moored our boat about eighty yards upwind of a nice looking bay whilst Doug and Dave anchored some fifty yards to our left. Our plan was rather to recce this deeper end of the Broad for future trips — than in the expectation of immediate action. But, within minutes, my herring float started moving quickly upwind against the waves.

It was a typical herring run on Broadland and I duly boated a scrappy pike of 9 lb 5 oz. A few minutes later my paternostered livebait was taken by a jack of about 4 lb. I recast to the same area, a little upwind of the boat, and about twenty minutes later the float bobbed under again: another 4 lb jack.

All the usual accusations of my being a jack basher just to beat them came echoing across with the wind from Doug and Dave. To rub salt into their wounds Martin's float, fishing a static herring, shot off. He brought a nice fish of 10 lb 6 oz to the net and we shouted back our score of four fish to none.

We then settled down to a long period of inactivity as the heavy rain started to fall and which continued for the remainder of the day. But Martin and I were pleased to have had some immediate action on a 'new' water. We moved several times downwind, towards where the deep water shelved abruptly up to just three feet, spending an hour at each anchorage without another run. Doug and Dave fared likewise and, around lunchtime, they moved over to the other side of the Broad where they stayed for the remainder of the day without a single run. For our last move of the day at about four p.m., I suggested that we row upwind and position the boat where our baits would be on the bottom close to the area where we first started. Martin agreed, and we put the anchor poles down a little to the right of our original area where the wind was now just slightly rippling the surface. It was nice to

Martin Page hoists a 20-pounder on to the scales

be out of the full blow despite there being little activity for about an hour. Then, quite suddenly, Martin said his float was away. I looked at the float which was not moving, then his line which was also not moving and put the landing net down. He remarked that the float was much further out than where he had cast it when, all of a sudden, a grebe popped up to the surface close to the float. After this grebe attack on Martin's herring, the float swung round in the wind to its original position as if to reassure us.

One of my floats was only a few yards away and I asked Martin to pull his in a bit, which, as it turned out was just as well, because he had, in fact had a run after all. The pike must have been lying doggo with the bait. He struck instantly and said that he was into a good fish. I grabbed the net again and started to clear the other rods for action when, quite suddenly, one of the anchor poles pulled out of the bottom and we swung round in the wind. Martin grabbed the landing net while I frantically paddled away with one oar to pull the boat back to its original position. We were in a muddle for a few minutes with lines all over the place — one being completely tangled up with the pike. Finally the fish was under control and Martin slipped the net underneath at the first attempt, and a very good fish it looked to be. He heaved it aboard and there lay a nicely-conditioned pike which just made the magical mark of 20 lb 4 oz and thirty-nine inches long. I took several photographs and we quickly sorted out the lines and general in the boat before putting out the baits again. We were all keyed up with that terrific optimism which, as on so many previous occasions, turned out to be quite unjustified. We sat there without another run until the sun broke through the rain clouds half an hour before we had to go. On their way back to the boat stagings Doug and Dave rowed over to see the fish before Martin returned it, and we followed them soon afterwards.

A very encouraging start on this 'new' water. We shall obviously go again shortly and, I think, concentrate on the deep water with the herrings. The pike certainly seem to like them here.

Sunday, 24 October

Light southerly wind, very sunny and warm from eight a.m. onwards.

My wife Barbara rarely comes fishing with me these days but, because I had arranged a last zander trip to the Relief Channel for this year with Terry

Houseago, Maureen and Nobby Clark, Dickie Dawson and other friends, she decided to forgo the usual Sunday lie-in and come along. We foregathered in Dereham and zipped along the Kings Lynn road towards the Channel to a new spot, which a friend had suggested might be worth a try, at Magdalen railway bridge.

This part of the Channel is more welcoming than my usual spot, further upstream at Downham, where the banks are steep with little in the way of reeds or rushes to soften the bleakness. It was nice to settle in between the clumps of tall Norfolk reeds and we had all the rods out with an assortment of live and deadbaits ledgered on the bottom not long after first light.

There was an enormous bream shoal moving on the surface, so large that those of us who fished near its centre were constantly experiencing line bites which, at first, we took to be finicky zander takes. When zander runs did occur, however, there was no mistaking them, and within the first hour, we accounted for seven fish between us, mostly between one and three pounds — the best $4^3/_4$ lb. Not exactly furious feeding considering that nine anglers were fishing two rods apiece over a stretch about 150 yards long. I think the strong sunlight which came early, due to a cloudless sky, did not help matters. By nine-thirty a.m. sport went completely dead except for my only two runs of the morning which came in quick succession a little later and were both missed. It was my first blank on the Channel for quite some time.

A pleasant morning, nevertheless. I must visit this particular stretch again for I am sure that, with a little study and good weather conditions, it could produce in the future. But that is for next year; I doubt I shall visit the Channel again this year as my thoughts are on piking and I am looking forward to this coming Thursday when I have promised Martin Page a trip to "the Conifers" Lake.

Tuesday, 26 October

Overcast morning, still, hint of rain, mild.

The clocks were put back one hour on Sunday, which means that daybreak now comes at a little after six. I decided this morning to have a couple of hours herring-bashing before work and paid a visit to Haveringland Lake. Some big pike have been taken from this shallow water over the past few seasons, mostly to static deadbaits. Being only six miles from home, the lake is a good alternative for my pre work sessions if the Wensum is in poor shape and the chances of roach are slim.

This morning I fished with herrings on both rods from six-thirty to eight-thirty without a run, though I think this quite mild weather has put these particular pike in a dour mood. There were plenty of small fish moving on the surface during my stay but not a single pike swirl in their wake. When there is a real bite to the weather and the bait shoals become packed together I think the pike will go on the rampage.

Thursday, 28 October

Continual fine drizzle accompanied by light NE wind, very overcast all day.

The almost continual rain of late has coloured most of my local rivers — the Wensum, in particular is high and of a brown hue: nice roaching conditions, in fact. So it was with mixed feelings that Martin Page and I visited "the Conifers" Lake this morning after the pike. As an insurance against poor sport I had asked Martin to bring his trotting rod along.

We were at the lake by dawn, and after loading up the boat with all the gear, I slowly rowed across a calm surface broken only by spots of drizzle and small fry towards my favourite pike area. From our anchorage close to the shore we fished the usual static herrings on slider floats well over depth, out towards the centre of the lake. After two hours of absolutely nothing we moved towards the middle and fanned the rods all around the boat to see if we could locate a taking area. There were small bream and roach continually moving on the surface and, every so often, a pike would swirl up and make its kill.

These attacks came from all over the lake and it rather seemed as though the pike were on the move well off the bottom and not interested in static, bottom-fished baits. So I dispensed with one of the floats and, after mounting a herring head first, started to wobble it at around midwater. On the second cast I felt a gentle take and gave line to a fish which very quickly swam off. It felt fairly heavy so I struck as soon as it had travelled a few yards. There was an immediate response and a nice fight followed from a spirited fish of 11 lb 9 oz.

A little while later I had another take on the wobble but the bait was rejected as I was about to strike. During this time Martin had accounted for a couple of jacks around the 5 lb mark (to a twitched bait beneath a float) and lost a double-figure fish which had snapped up a static (our only take to statics) quite close to the boat.

Martin was a little disappointed for I had told him of how these particular lake fish can go and he was just starting to enjoy the fight when the hooks pulled free. A pity — the fish looked all of 14 lb — plus. After this initial feeding spell all went quiet for a while and even the small fry dotting the surface were left alone. We repeatedly cast our statics out to different spots around the boat, whilst wobbling with the spare rods, to see if the pike were still moving — which they were not. Then, quite suddenly, as I tightened my line after putting a static out, the float bobbed and shot off before the herring had reached the bottom. A pike — and a good one at that — had nobbled it as it fluttered down through fourteen feet of water. I struck quickly and there was an immediate response. The fish shot to the surface way out, thrashed about, and dived down deep where I was pleased to let it slog around for a few

A 15lbs 10oz pike

minutes while Martin put up the net (we always keep it folded away until required for ease of movement in the boat).

As I pumped it towards the boat it zoomed up to the surface and showered us in a cloud of spray before diving deep again. The power of these pike is really incredible and I had to pull out all the stops to keep it away from the anchor lines beneath the boat. A couple more heavy runs followed and then Martin quickly slipped the net under it before it could dive again. It was a very long fish which fought like a thirty-pounder is supposed to, but which weighed 15 lb 10 oz. How I wish I could connect with a twenty-plus fish from this lake — the fight would really be something to remember.

This last spot of action brought the time up to midday and, after another hour of inactivity, I mentioned to Martin that, instead of waiting for the dusk feeding spell, we could spend the remainder of the afternoon back at the Wensum which looked promising, the river being so coloured. I wished, afterwards, that I had kept my mouth shut.

We fished from two o'clock until dark at the rushes — the river in superb trim — but with just one roach of a pound to my rod on maggots. The only bite of the afternoon.

I had expected the roach to be queueing up for baits and to take, at the very least, several good roach apiece. Whether the flood water had soured their appetites (there was much rubbish drifting down) or not, I do not know. The Wensum here has been in a most peculiar mood since my catches of last summer and winter, or perhaps the roach have simply moved much further upstream and are not in such numbers as they were.

I felt rather guilty dragging Martin away from the possibility of pike at "the Conifers" for absolutely nothing at the Wensum.

Thursday, 4 November

Overnight frost followed by a cold westerly wind.

Worthing gravel pit, which lies fifteen miles due west of Norwich close to the upper Wensum, is an irregular shaped water of some seven acres. In places the bottom contours shelve down over twenty feet deep, the average being fourteen feet. Being open to wind and rather bleak it was not really the sort of place to fish for pike on this, the coldest day of this winter. At least, that's how Doug Allen and I felt as we made our way at dawn along winding roads, with a crisp carpet of frost covering the almost lifeless countryside. On arrival at the pit the enthusiasm for pike fishing soon came back and we quickly slid the dinghy off the trailer into the water which was, thank goodness, free of ice.

Not having boat fished here before, we decided to plumb for the middle to find our first anchorage and to fan rods all around the boat, fishing our favourite static herrings on each. We expected sport to be slow, but, within about fifteen minutes, one of my floats popped under and line quickly disappeared from the spool. This was quite promising for a first trip, and I hit into a fish which felt quite solid, despite it being at least fifty yards away from the boat as the hooks went home. After a spirited fight, I played the fish out to the side of the boat and guided it into Doug's waiting net. Not as big as I had first thought, tipping the scales at 13 lb 7 oz; nevertheless, a good 'first' fish.

Within minutes of returning it (unless it is really large and worth photographing we always return pike immediately) one of Doug's floats shot off and he too connected with a 'nice one' which tried to get under the boat. But after losing two fish to the anchor ropes a fortnight ago at "the Conifers", Doug turned it in time and allowed it to slog away from the boat while I put the net up again. After a really good scrap Doug brought the pike alongside and I heaved it into the boat. It was very long, lean fish with a nasty red wound on one jaw (bad unhooking by someone else) weighing one ounce more than mine.

These two instant fish did wonders for our optimism and, for the next two hours, I think we were both expecting a run at any moment, but I suppose that would have been too easy. None came, and we up-anchored to move further downwind towards the end where the Wensum runs alongside the pit.

After a few minutes at our new position, Doug had a run from a goodish fish, certainly another 'double', but which came adrift after a few seconds. Then I felt a pike grab my herring close to the bottom on the wobble, but after allowing it a few yards before striking, it promptly let go as I was about to set the hooks. It is strange how pike will eject a deadbait when grabbed on the move but rarely if fished static.

I put both baits out on the bottom after that and very shortly boated a jack of about 5 lb, on the static again. Then Doug missed a run because he picked up the wrong rod and his strike must have moved the line with the pike on (the floats were quite close together). From the size of the teeth marks on the herring it was another jack, anyway.

We moved again at two p.m. to our last anchorage of the day, slightly upwind of the spot where we had first started. But we ended, quietly, without another run.

The pit certainly seems an early-morning venue when fishing static

137

The first double-figure pike from a new water

herrings — if just one trip is enough to judge by. Perhaps the cold conditions, coupled with the fact that as the day lengthened the westerly wind freshened, put the pike in a torpid mood.

The water is certainly worth some future trips, perhaps on a mild, wet day with a south-west wind. These are the sort of conditions both Doug and I always seem to do well in, particularly with static herring.

Saturday, 6 November

Very overcast, slight drizzle accompanied by light Northerly wind.

I fished the Rushes stretch of the Wensum this morning for an hour before work in the hope that my dace livebaits might attract one of those large pike that inhabit the bushes and the end swims.

If any were still in residence they certainly were not in a feeding mood. Only the jacks were active and in the short period between seven a.m. and eight a.m. I hooked into four fish, all below 5 lb, landing just one which I put

138

into the dyke running alongside the river. I am thinking in terms of some more good roaching sessions for this coming winter so a few less jacks will not harm the river which is starting to look in good order.

I think the very next bout of prolonged rain will see the roach feeding if accompanied by mild conditions.

Thursday, 11 November

Freezing fog from first light till ten a.m. followed by strong sunlight for remainder of the day.

Doug Allen and I had planned a piking trip to "the Conifers" lake for today but, when I rang yesterday to book the water, the owner informed me that he was in the middle of his annual bird count (water fowl) and that the lake would not be free until next week. So we changed to a roaching session on the Wensum at the Rushes which, as it turned out, was a lucky break.

However, when we arrived at dawn with a chilling fog hugging a quickly moving but low river, I was not optimistic. The only good thing was that due to heavy rain in the past few days the Wensum had a nice smokey colour to it. We walked upstream to the top of the fishery where I chose the top glide swim and Doug settled in at the bushes, eighty yards downstream. I catapulted a few maggots to the head of the swim and fished two on a size 16 fine wire spade end beneath a 3AA peacock quill.

After half an hour of exploring the centre channel, dragging the maggots close to the bottom, everything seemed dead except that a few good roach were priming on the surface well below the swim and close to the far bank. I allowed the float to trot down much further on my next cast and, quite suddenly as it neared the surface activity, it shot under. I struck and a nice roach boiled before diving and zooming upstream towards me, where I bullied it into the landing net. It was about $1^1/_2$ lb and a good start.

I kept feeding in maggots and expected more bites but the roach seemed loth to follow them upstream so I crept downstream and tried a swim through directly opposite where the roach were swirling. The float went just two yards and sunk positively. A good roach thumped the rod tip a couple of times and then rolled off. I feared this might have spooked the others but on the very next cast, after I had moved the keep net to this new spot, a quick bite resulted in another good roach of about $1^3/_4$ lb. More bites followed in a short, hectic feeding spell and I took another four good fish, all between $1^1/_2$

lb and $1^3/_4$ lb before connecting with the first two-pounder of the winter; 2 lb $1^1/_2$ oz to be exact.

In the meantime, Doug had wandered up after missing the only two bites at the bush swim. But he said that some good fish were moving on the surface in the long glide downstream of the bush so, after having a cup of tea, he took off downstream whilst I commenced trotting down. A few casts later I hit into a really big fish which took right in front of me, and for several minutes I prayed that the 16 hook would not come out. These Wensum roach really motor when in winter trim, sometimes taking several yards of line in boring runs, and this fish was no exception. It seemed ages before I saw its head break surface downstream and carefully I pumped it up along the margin to the already sunken net. A steady lift and he was on the bank. An old looking fish — over sixteen inches long — which at some time during its life must have weighed a few ounces more than its current 2 lb 9 oz. I shouted down to Doug that I was still taking them — to which he shouted back that so was he.

I had two more bites during the next hour which brought the time up to around ten o'clock. One I missed, the other was from another nice roach of 1

Douglas Allen bringing in a 2lb roach

lb 14 oz. After this the sun broke through the mist — which it had been threatening to do — and the swim went dead.

I was quite happy though — jubilant, in fact, and decided to wander down to see how Doug was faring. He was really taking fish and had been since his first trot down. He had two in the net, amongst half a dozen, which looked to be over the 2 lb mark and he added another within seconds of my sitting down amongst the rushes alongside. Unlike my swim, where the action was fast and furious but short lived, Doug was really having to work hard for every fish in this long glide. Bites came from no particular area; the float would suddenly shoot under, sometimes right in front of him, sometimes twenty yards downstream. But more amazing was that the roach were still feeding despite the strong sunlight and flat calm conditions. While Doug carried on taking the odd fish, I roamed the whole fishery during the next few hours — spending half an hour in each swim to see if I could connect with a shoal, but without so much as a touch. Every so often I popped back to Doug's swim to find that he was still having the occasional bites.

At about three o'clock, with an hour of daylight left, my trotting arm was aching so I decided to roam no more and to sit beside Doug who, as I approached from a last fling at the top glide, was fast into a big roach. As he guided it over the net, I swore it was larger than his previous best roach of 2 lb 5 oz taken here in February. And it was — a lovely deep roach in absolute mint condition weighing 2 lb 6$\frac{1}{2}$ oz.

Doug's face lit up and he suddenly had a little sympathy for poor old Wilson not having had a bite since ten o'clock. He suggested that I might as well creep into the rushes a few yards downstream of him for a final fling. "Don't go and get another big one though" said Doug, at which I laughed and promptly struck into a good fish of 2 lb 2$\frac{1}{2}$ oz on the very first trot down. I did not tell Doug that it was a fluke till we got home: I had actually hooked it in the eye. Right in the middle of the eye itself, my first eye-hooked big roach. My first eye-hooked anything, come to think of it.

As the light faded away and mist started to roll off the meadows along the margins we took one more fish apiece both about 1$\frac{1}{2}$ lb and then called it a day. What a day's roaching it had been! We have both caught lots more roach at a sitting before, but few catches have contained roach of such a high average size. When we lifted the nets out we noticed that every single fish, except for my long one, was quite young-looking and, for the time of year, very deep-chested. They were, in fact, in far nicer shape than when we fished here in February. So, with three months of the season yet to go, they should fill out even more — perhaps even to 3 lb.

Happy, as only a day's long trotting and a catch of prime roach can make you, we trudged wearily back to the car, feeling more than pleased that my dark suspicions of the river over the past few months had been totally unjustified.

Summary of the day's catch

Doug: 15 roach — four over 2 lb; the best being 2 lb 6$^1/_2$ oz.
Myself: 10 roach — three over 2 lb; the best being 2 lb 9 oz.
Total weight: almost fifty pounds.

Saturday, 13 November

Overcast, mild, hint of rain.

After Thursday's wonderful roach sport, I decided to visit the "Rushes" again this morning for a couple of hours trotting before work.

Unfortunately, and due to the heavy rain of yesterday, the Wensum was near to full flood making trotting down only just possible. I tried two swims, the top glide and the long glide where Doug took his catch on Thursday, but without a bite.

Sunday, 14 November

Overcast, no wind, quite mild.

When I finally arrived on the Wensum at the "Rushes" stretch at ten-thirty this morning it was still roaring down, chocolate in colour, and unfishable. Just as well really for I would have kicked myself had I missed out on the nice weather conditions. Actually, the weather forecast was for a freezing fog and sub zero temperatures and I was most surprised when exactly the opposite had greeted my first sleepy look through the bedroom curtains.

Whenever the Wensum is unfishable the nearby, and usually gin clear, river Tud always has a little colour and produces some sport. So I visited a very winding stretch of the river in Ringland Hills for a spot of dacing. It was nice to fish in an unhurried way for a few hours, not expecting to catch anything special, and the dozen or so dace up to about 6 oz from a deepish bend gave me an appetite for lunch.

They came to trotted maggots at first and then on the bottom when I pushed the float up to stret peg. I also took a small brown trout and lost a fair chub.

A relaxing session.

Thursday, 18 November

Very overcast, exceptionally mild, no wind.

Having fined down nicely over the past few days, the river Wensum looked most inviting this morning as Doug Allen and I crept quietly along the bank at dawn towards our favourite roach swims. What with overcast and mild conditions, coupled with the water holding some colour, I would have put money on our taking some nice roach.

Doug fished the bush swim and, after about ten minutes, latched onto a very big roach approaching the $2^1/_2$ lb mark — only to lose it close to the net; the hook link snapping as the roach made a last-second dive for freedom. Shortly afterwards, fishing about sixty yards below Doug, I managed to connect with a roach of around 12 oz which also nearly came adrift (thanks to a pike appearing from nowhere) but which missed in its excitement.

These were our only bites from roach. We roamed the entire stretch for four hours trying to contact a shoal by leapfrogging from swim to swim, spending half an hour in each. It really was most strange under such seemingly perfect conditions.

I had been dubious about the actual number of roach still in residence at the "Rushes" all this summer. Until last Thursday, when we took that large bag, I was of the impression that, compared to last winter, few roach were about. After this morning's session I am heading back towards the same conclusion that after their close-season spawning activities upriver only a small percentage (albeit very large fish) have so far returned to the "Rushes" stretch.

Before leaving at lunchtime to try for some roach action on the upper Yare, at Bawburgh, I could not resist bunging out a livebait to try for the pike in my swim. I had brought a few with me, just in case, and it was just as well. A plump seven-pounder quickly grabbed a small dace just a few yards downstream from where it had swirled earlier. He will not disturb us there again for I put him in the dyke behind the river to annoy the dace instead of the big roach.

Like the Wensum, the upper Yare was nicely coloured and flowing strongly with, in complete contrast to the Wensum, fish feeding in almost every swim. We roamed along a half-mile length of this little river exploring each interesting bend and glide, taking nothing special — though Doug did lose a biggish chub whilst trotting alongside a raft on the opposite bank. It shot under the raft into dense flood rubbish and, on a size 16 hook to $1^1/_2$ lb line, Doug could do nothing to stop it.

Our catch included lots of small roach and dace, a perch of about half a pound and three roach all on the pound mark. We felt our move from the Wensum had been justified although, when you set out in the morning after big fish and full of optimism, a scratching session comes a poor second. I think we both finished the day a trifle frustrated that our preconceived idea that excellent conditions should always produce just rewards was wrong.

Sunday, 21 November

Chilly overcast morning, no wind.

I failed to hear the alarm clock this morning set for six-thirty a.m. and so a planned roaching session was wasted. Nevertheless, after breakfast I took my son Lee along to the "Rushes" for a short livebaiting session. It had to be short because I could net only three dace from my pond (I must replenish the stock very soon).

We tried several swims, trotting the baits close to the bottom before the first run, which resulted in Lee's first pike of about five pounds. I had to set the hooks for him but then handed over the rod to reel off a few shots on the camera. He thoroughly enjoyed the session and could have taken another jack if it had not spat the bait out as I was about to assemble the net.

The river has really run off now after the flooding and is back to being low and very clear. Not a sign of roach moving.

Thursday, 25 November

Overcast all day, a moderate westerly wind, quite mild.

Doug Allen and I have just returned from a day's piking at "the Conifers" Lake where sport was fast and furious, to say the least. In fact, I cannot ever remember having so many runs or catching so many pike before.

Every pike in the lake seemed to be on the move and, within minutes of lowering the anchors about sixty yards from the leeward bank, we cast our herring baits downwind into the middle of the lake and the fun started.

Here, in about fifteen feet of water, our static herrings were taken greedily in bolting runs and almost within minutes we both had fish on at once. Doug's came adrift (his only lost fish of the day as it turned out) and mine weighed just 5 lb. While I was untangling one of the hooks from the landing net the other line (a freelined bait) popped out of the rubber band on the rod handle and hissed from the reel in a blurr. I left Doug to deal with the net and struck.

This fish felt much better and, when half way in, shot quickly upwards to tail walk across the surface: a beautiful sight. It then dived again and remained deep, making several heavy, very fast, runs. After nearly losing it around the anchor rope I finally managed to put the net under a very long fish with a peculiar round scar along one flank. I recognised it as the very same pike I had caught two weeks ago when fishing here with Martin Page. Then it weighed 15 lb 10 oz but had since lost weight and barely made 15 lb. Very soon after this, Doug connected with a good "double" (again on the static herring) which weighed 14 lb: another long, extremely powerful fish. Within minutes one of my lines was again streaking out through the rod rings. I immediately realised that another "double" had taken a liking to our herrings as it kited at speed to my left and went round the back of the boat where I was pleased to let it slog away down deep, well away from the other lines. Doug did a good job of the netting at the first attempt and I logged a sixteen-pounder.

We settled down yet again but, after just two sips from my cup of tea, I was off again. This time it was the float rod, fishing a static herring. When I struck there must have been at least sixty yards of line out and yet the pike, staying deep, still felt very heavy. I pumped it in slowly — very slowly indeed — and, as it neared the boat, I caught a glimpse of a really deep flank through the clear water. Then the bait popped out of its mouth. I was sick because I was sure that fish was close to the twenty-pounder that we have yet to hook from the lake.

I wound the bait in to inspect the hooks which were sound. Then I heard a muffled crack, followed by a popping sound. It came from the spool which split apart, and a hundred yards of new line came off in a huge spiral. This cheered Doug who went off into one of his uncontrollable fits of laughter. "Serves you right" he said — hinting that, for a tackle dealer, my gear was rather neglected. I suppose there was some truth in this, but the reason for the

Counting up the roach

spool splitting was my cramming a hundred yards of 9 lb line on to a "medium" Mitchell spool (which is plastic) instead of the "deep" metal spool. I suspect that the pressure from pumping the last fish in was just too much for it.

After swapping spools we had well over thirty minutes without a run — about our only lull of the day. The pike then started moving again to our statics, wobbled baits, and even freelined baits which were taken before they had time to hit the bottom. In a hectic spell, lasting a good twenty minutes, there was not a single moment when either one or both of us were not playing or unhooking a fish. I think we boated eight fish during this time and lost three but I cannot be sure for there was so much going on. We weighed the best two — both around 10 lb. The others ranged from about 3 lb to 8 lb, and this type of action was to last the whole day through.

We moved twice — across the wind in the hope of finding an area where only larger fish were situated. I think we both suspected that, on a day when every pike in the lake seemed to be stocking up for a hard winter, that the Conifers "twenty" would at last show up.

But it did not, though we took fish of nearly every other weight. We even boated a few really tiny jacks of 2 lb which took small wobbled sprats with real gusto, and shook others off the hooks rather than unnecessarily untangle

146

Into a good pike

trebles from the landing net. In all we accounted for some twenty-eight pike with about another dozen lost — all, except one, by me. Still it was a fabulous day's fishing which included nine double-figure fish to 16 lb.

Because the action was so furious and we did not mind losing one because another soon grabbed hold, I was constantly picking up the camera and rolling off as many action shots as possible, using two 20 exposure rolls in the process. I cannot wait to get them developed, there should be some beautiful shots of Doug leaning over the boat grimly holding onto a double-figure pike bent on wrapping the trace around the anchor ropes. But luckily, despite our casual approach, not a single fish managed to go completely under the boat; though how, I do not know.

Sunday, 28 November

Overcast, strong westerly wind with heavy rain at times.

Nobby Clarke and I have often discussed whether angling photographs would turn out more natural and better composed if, when we go after something specific, one did the fishing and the other concentrated on the photography.

This morning session we planned to put our theory into practice and also to compare the merits of our favourite single lens reflex 35 mm cameras and the larger, heavier $2^1/_4''$ square twin lens when taking action shots along the overgrown banks of a small river while after chub. We decided that Nobby would concentrate on shooting film whilst I tried to produce some fish. However after a lengthy Saturday night dinner and dance, I had only been in bed for three hours when the alarm clock rang accompanied by a bang on the front door from Nobby. To make the thought of crawling along muddy banks even more distasteful, when I opened the door heavy rain lashed into the hallway from a force 6 gale.

Nevertheless, we were soon speeding along the Bungay road towards the upper Waveney — my favourite chubbing river. We planned to fish a very overgrown stretch near Homersfield where alder trees and willows overhang the bendy swims, providing good cover for the sizeable chub lying beneath. As we were early I suggested that it might be worth trying first two known chub swims at Bungay Common, which was en route.

Just as dawn was breaking we crept up to the first swim, where a huge willow tree hangs out over the water and settled in amongst the dying rushes about twenty yards upstream. I threw in a few free samples of bread flake alongside the low lying branches where flood water debris had formed a raft and rigged up a link ledger holding two swan shot.

The strong wind and heavy rain made accurate casting a nightmare and I lost two ledger rigs in the willow before the bait landed just right and swung down through the clear water under the raft. Within seconds, almost, I felt a slight tightening on my index finger holding the line, followed by a quick tap on the rod tip. I struck — prematurely — and missed it. I lobbed out another piece of flake to the same spot and again, within seconds of the bait finding bottom, there was a similar bite which I hit on the second knock and the hook went home. Nobby started clicking away with his $2^1/_4$" square the very second I bent into the chub, which came belting upriver where I quickly put the net under it: a $2^1/_2$ — pounder.

Due to the bad light which necessitated using flash unit, Nobby found that focusing and winding-on after each shot was a slow process and that, in cramped conditions where quick camera adjustments are an absolute must if you want to capture all the action, the SLR 35 mm would have been better.

I had a couple more casts under the raft without any takes so we moved below the willow to the next bend where the branches of an alder bush formed another chub raft. Keeping well upstream, behind a clump of reeds, I threw in some more free bait and, after a few minutes wait to allow the chub to find them, cast in. Just like the first swim, an immediate bite brought another $2^1/_2$ lb chub. But there was nothing else — the gin clear water put paid to that, so we loaded up the car again and made for Homersfield.

The rain was becoming a nuisance, especially for Nobby who really needed both cameras at the ready for the slightest sign of a fish. And they had to be cased, as our approach to the first swim (another alder bush raft) meant crawling the last muddy yards through brambles so as not to scare the chub. I flicked in some more free bait close to the near bank just up from the alder. Nobby demisted his glasses and the camera view finder and I delayed casting a piece of freeline flake until he was set up. This was just as well for the line tightened and the rod tip yanked round before the bait hit bottom. Another instant chub which lunged heavily beneath the raft and put a good curve in my avon 11-footer. All good action stuff for Nobby, who took several sequence shots on the 35 mm SLR from the hooking to netting of a short, plump fish of 3 lb 1 oz which I slipped in well upstream before tackling the next swim downstream. This was a nightmare of a chub hole where a dry ditch joins the main flow creating a cup in the bank. To make a cast by lowering bait through a small hole in the middle of an alder bush means crawling on all fours through two sets of barbed wire. Once in position, nasty hawthorns growing on either side of the ditch form a dense roof overhead and the only way to rebait is to push the rod backwards until you can reach the hook, wound up to within six inches of the rod tip. Nobby thought I was barmy, but crawled through and sat in the ditch behind me shielding the cameras from the rain.

After freebaiting some flake I opened the bale arm and allowed the current to take my piece of flake downstream to rest on the bottom three yards away in three feet of water. After several minutes the rod tip pulled round an inch and I replied by winding in like mad and pulling the rod. Even then the hook landed in the alder branches because I missed the bite. I missed another bite on the next cast and then, after much cursing, I hooked into something. It was not a chub but a good roach which boiled on the surface a second before the line snapped at the reel. I quickly shoved the rod behind me and grabbed the last foot before it passed through the tip ring. Netting it, with one hand

A good roach from the chub hole

holding the rod and the other grasping both line and net handle, was a bit tricky but providing more good stuff for Nobby. It was not a bad roach, either, a fraction below $1^3/_4$ lb.

No more bites followed — which was not surprising considering the commotion I made — and we trudged off downstream to try some more swims. All seemed barren of chub except one — another alder bush swim. When I set the hook to my last bite of the morning, even that turned out to be another goodish roach of $1^1/_4$ lb.

Like a couple of drowned rats and covered in mud, we trudged wearily back to the car to be home in time for lunch. Although we did not contact any big chub — in such bad conditions — three chub and two good roach were more than we expected. At least Nobby had shot off two rolls of film and found that for creeping and crawling photography the 35 mm SLR take some beating.

Thursday, 2 December

Overcast, bitterly cold, Northerly wind (strong at times) accompanied by rain showers.

Today I fished the same deep broad near Horning which produced a few fish including that $20^1/_4$ — pound pike for Martin Page several weeks ago. But how fortunes can change in a few weeks!

When David Broome and I arrived at half past seven this morning, we immediately noticed how clear the water was and I remarked there and then that our prospects of taking much on herrings in such clear water conditions, let alone in freezing cold weather, was remote. Unfortunately, I was right.

We stuck it out till one p.m. without a single run, and I was a little sad for David because, whenever we have fished together during the past few years, we have fared badly. In fact, David only came along today to keep me company as Doug Allen is off to Wales for a fortnight's chubbing on the Wye. When we trudged back to the car after six hours of shivering in the vain hope of our herring floats moving we both wished we had stayed at home.

AFTERTHOUGHTS

I hope today's fishing is not a bad omen (snow is falling as I write) for this coming weekend. My brother David is paying a visit in the hope that he can enjoy some good sport. I have booked "the Conifers" for a pike trip — so we shall see.

Sunday, 5 December

Sub-zero temperatures for the entire day, a light westerly wind, extremely sharp frost, really cold.

Just as I thought — brother Dave's chances of catching anything worthwhile this weekend were once again blighted by weather conditions. He really has been unlucky when fishing in Norfolk this year, both summer and winter.

We rose early this morning at six-thirty a.m. to find the promised frost carpeting the front lawn and half an inch of ice over the pond. It was just as well that we had extracted a dozen livebait from it last night and kept them in a bucket with an oxygen pump, otherwise our bait would have consisted only of herrings.

After a careful drive over slippery roads we arrived at "the Conifers" Lake just as dawn was breaking to find that almost all the lake was iced up. This immediately ruled out boat fishing and the chance of Dave piking the most productive area, but there was an ice-free patch by the outlet dyke — which meant that we could fish, at least. It was either here or back to the Wensum (which was roaring down) for a chancy session. So we chose the long walk around the lake through, an almost primitive looking scene of gnarled old conifer trees laden down with thick frost, to the outlet dyke. We had to break back some dead foliage at the outlet to make a clearing large enough for casting but within half an hour we had four rods out — two on static herrings and two fishing paternostered livebaits.

I thought at first that, despite our constricted bankside position, we might be able to reach the edge of the boat fishing area, but after a short walk around the lake where I could see the limited range of our floats despite long casting, I could see we were nowhere near it. Distance fishing is always deceptive until the cast is seen sideways on. Nevertheless, we did manage to pick up four small fish from 4 to $8^{1}/_{2}$ lb on the paternostered baits but without a single run on the herrings. The lake has become quite clear during the past week of continual frosts — not good herring conditions; I always like a tinge of colour when presenting statics.

As the morning lengthened and our time for departure drew near the air temperature actually decreased and a thin layer of ice appeared over the water inside the livebait bucket. Not the sort of session I had planned for Dave but at least we had not blanked.

Thursday, 9 December

Sub-zero temperatures all day despite sunshine from midday till dusk, raw, north-westerly wind.

This cold spell of sharp nights and daytime frosts seems to be hanging on, making any thoughts of roaching or stillwater piking before Christmas fairly remote. In fact, even chub fishing is off at present as Vic Bellars and I found out today. We spent four miserable hours on the Wensum without a touch, and another three hours on the Upper Yare near Bawburgh with just a few tentative bites to our ledgered bread and cheese paste baits.

The only fish of the day was a pike of about half-a-pound which gobbled up a cube of crust the very instant my ledger hit bottom. But we don't count pike when we are chubbing so Vic and I had to log a blank session.

Thursday, 16 December

Very cold morning — no wind.

Although the cold weather still prevails, when I looked out through the front door at dawn this morning there was little ground frost about, and so I decided to go along to the rushes for a couple of hours.

The Wensum was pathetically low and running clear, but I could not resist an hours trotting to see if the roach were in a feeding mood — which, of course, they were not. There was no sign of a fish showing on the surface or down below after my maggots, so to save a silly blank morning I upped and drove through Ringland Hills to the river Tud for a spot of dacing.

Like the Wensum, the Tud was very cold looking but with a tinge of greeny-blue in the two deepish holes I tried. The first, a tiny back eddy on the outside of an acute bend, produced two dace of about 8 oz apiece with another one of around the same size lost. When bites ceased I moved downstream to where gnarled old alder trees lined both banks and met overhead, forming a nice tunnel-swim. There was a four-foot deep gulley close to the near bank at this spot, close to the alder roots where I have, on previous occasions, taken some really fine dace up to the 12 oz mark.

However, on my very first trot down something quite different sucked in the double maggots tripping bottom. At first I suspected a big trout but it was moving too slowly and kept low down, where it stayed for a few minutes, while I prayed for the size 16 hook not to come out. I could do nothing but hang on for several minutes, I managed to steer it away from the alder roots as it tried to reach the undercuts beneath. It was obviously a biggish chub but, due to my impatience and cold hands, I failed to find out. In an effort to prise it away from the roots and to have a look at what I had hooked it suddenly woke up and made a headlong dash right under the bank, snapping the line above the hook. Nevertheless, I had come for the dace so I stayed put and started trotting again.

After about twenty minutes, the float dipped slightly at the end of the swim and a nice dace was on. It fought quite spiritedly for its 10 oz but felt ridiculously small compared with the lost chub.

Before I left the swim and made tracks for work I had one more bite which resulted in a brown trout of about $1\frac{1}{2}$ lb. It put up a hell of a scrap — jumping and thrashing about — before slipping the hook as I was about to net it.

An interesting few hours and, if the cold weather continues over the weekend, I could do a lot worse than spend Sunday morning on the Tud. The dace are always good and I cannot resist having another go for that chub; but on heavier gear.

Sunday, 19 December

Bitterly cold, strong north easterly wind, overcast with occasional rain showers.

I do not know why, but whenever Nobby Clarke and I arrange a fishing trip the weather is invariably lousy, and this morning certainly proved no exception. In fact, had I been going alone I would have stayed in bed, but there outside the front door at the crack of dawn, accompanied by a howling, freezing-cold wind, was Nobby, festooned with cameras and tackle, all set for a photography — cum — fishing trip on the river Tud.

Like a fool, I had assured him of some action after my brief session on Thursday, though when we arrived to find the river badly swollen and thickly coloured and with lots of rubbish drifting down, I wished I had kept my big mouth shut. But a challenge is a challenge. Anyway, I was rather interested in fishing that undercut bank swim where Thursday's chub had unfairly broken my line and so, after showing Nobby the 'back eddy' swim further upstream, I walked back to the undercut and stret pegged a couple of maggots on the bottom in the now turbulent water close into the bank.

After a few minutes the float twitched and sat up as if to go under — but did not. Sucked maggots obviously meant a dace which did not seem to want to pull too hard in the icy water. In fact, the Tud was flooding with melted snow from a heavy fall on Friday and must have been out of sorts, because the dace in these fast swims usually bite very boldly. After rebaiting and positioning the float very close in to the bank I had another bite, but not from a dace. The float just cocked and sank all in one go and I was suddenly playing a chub — which, despite being no monster, really fought well, helped along no doubt by the extra-strong current. I was glad that I had tied the 14 hook direct to $2^1/_2$ lb reel line instead of my usual lighter hook length — otherwise there might have been a repeat performance of Thursday. It weighed about $2^1/_2$ lb I suppose — I was far too cold to get out the scales, and after returning it upstream I flogged the swim for another half hour without so much as a twitch. I then took a stroll up to Nobby for a chat and a cup of his tea — I always forget my flask on the coldest of days. He duly obliged and mumbled something about having a sucked maggot, the closest thing to a fish as yet.

The river was in a bad shape, and I could not understand why the dace in Nobby's swim were not in the slack formed by the back eddy. The only other piece of slack water in the swim was a small gap between the alder bushes on the outside of the bend and, with Nobby's permission, I crept round to lower the tackle through the branches almost under my feet. 'You won't get one there, Wilson' said Nobby — but the dace knew better and had, as I suspected, been sheltering from the force of the dirty water beneath the alder branches. I pulled out of the first fish, a good dace, and managed to hold onto the second as it thrashed around in the tangle of branches while Nobby ran round with the net. It was a nice fish of just over 10 oz with a pronounced early-spawning hump.

But that was the end of it, apart from a little brownie of around half a pound, and we gladly packed up the gear at noon and trudged back through the rain to the car.

Thursday, 23 December

Mild, overcast, windless morning.

When I woke at dawn this morning to find the air temperature had actually risen a few degrees I could not resist a roaching session at the rushes.

Conditions could not have been better with the Wensum back to normal level and nicely coloured — but oh those crafty roach! Where they were I just do not know. I tried four different swims, trotting maggots close to the bottom, without a single bite. The only piece of action to break the monotony came from a little stoat which must have been day dreaming on its morning walk. He trotted along to within a couple of yards of where I sat before he realised something was up. He then stood perfectly still, twitched his head from side to side as if to reassure himself that I wasn't a rabbit, and then turned round and shot off through the bracken. Lovely little fellows, stoats — almost dapper in their chestnut fur, with white bibs and bushy tails. It is a pity they have to go around eating all the other furry little creatures.

Monday, 27 December

Cold northerly wind, bright sunshine.

Barbara allowed me to escape from the seasonal festivities this morning. How nice it was to escape the Christmas hubbub of the kids fighting over their presents and the television blaring away for a few silent hours on the river.

Not that all this racket happens at six-thirty in the morning, of course, which was when I called round for Nobby Clarke who also fancied a roaching session. Wisely, we decided to visit the upper Waveney at Earsham where, even during the worst of conditions, catching a few fish is always on the cards. In fact, the river was in really fine shape — flowing strongly and nicely coloured — with fish feeding in almost every swim we tried despite a bitterly cold northerly wind. We caught nothing special; I suppose the best roach scaled a little over $1^1/_4$ lb but, with another six over the pound amongst a combined bag of about thirty fish, we were more than pleased.

This part of the Waveney has almost completely recovered from the national roach decline of the late sixties, and has huge quantities of small fish. It is a most heartwarming sight, and while the presence of more fish in the river does make contacting the elusive two-pounders far more difficult, getting plenty of bites when the weather is foul is a nice bonus.

In fact, this morning's session really sharpened our reflexes for tomorrow when there is an event to which I am looking forward. It is a match between a team of local matchmen most of whom are members of the Norwich National team and captained by Roger Harris against the Norwich Specimen Hunters, captained by yours truly. It's an event which creates a large amount of local interest and enthusiasm because it was held for the first time last year as a direct result of a controversy which raged for several weeks in the angling page of the *Eastern Evening News*. All sorts of arguments were put forward to prove that specimen hunters were more skilful than match men, or vice versa. In the end everyone came to the conclusion that different skills are required to succeed in each branch of fishing. However, the *Eastern Evening News* generously decided to sponsor a match between the two sides with a trophy for the winners and plenty of free pints at the local for everyone after the match. We specimen hunters lost, of course. No, that's wrong — we were massacred, we caught only 30 lb of fish to the matchmen's tally of over 80 lb. In fact, their top man, Stan Karn, actually beat our overall weight by himself by netting over 40 lb. All except one member of our seven-man team caught fish. Several huge roach showed up — the largest, weighing $2^1/_2$ lb, fell to the rod of one of our team, David Gowing who also notched up our best weight of $14^1/_2$ lb.

So tomorrow should prove quite interesting again, providing the temperature doesn't fall too low overnight. We do not really expect to win against such expert match anglers, of course, but I suppose anything can happen, depending on the draw, because the match is a pegged down affair starting at eight a.m. and finishing at noon.

Tuesday, 28 December

Exceptionally sharp overnight frost followed by bright sunshine from nine a.m., no wind.

What I cannot stand about match fishing is that if you draw a dead swim you still have to go through the motions for the entire match, knowing full well that the chance of a bite, let alone a fish, is quite remote. That was my misfortune today, but luckily I wasn't alone — only two of our eight-man contingent managed to pluck out a few fish from a particularly cold, clear and slow-flowing river Yare. Needless to say, we lost again — only this time by a much greater margin than last year, although the overall weights for both teams were much lower due to the conditions. Roger's matchmen accounted for 30 lb of (mainly) roach and small dace to our paltry 1 lb 10 oz. It was a thrashing and didn't I take some stick at the weigh-in? But I have got a thick skin and have learned to take it all in good part.

At the pub after the match, where the editor of the *Eastern Evening News* presented Roger's team with their well-deserved trophy, we all had an inquest about where we went wrong. One of their team, David Roe, actually scaled down to a $^3/_4$ lb hook length and size 20 hook to amass a catch of 68 small dace to weigh in just over 2 lb. In the cold conditions, with an overnight drop in temperature to minus 4 degrees centigrade, we found that only this super-light tackle would succeed. Not that I shall ever scale down so drastically, because I wouldn't expect to land a big roach from the Wensum on a size 20 hook, but I shall certainly rethink my terminal tackle for next year's match if the temperatures are sub-zero. There is the consolation that whatever the conditions we cannot possibly lose by a greater margin than that of today.

In many ways I think today's blank and the others which have cropped up just lately during this spell of exceedingly low temperatures make a fitting end to this year. I would have loved to have gone out with a big-un, but as the year started so beautifully due to such settled weather conditions it is perhaps only fair to accept that, unless water and weather conditions are right, catching anything (let alone specimen fish) is far from predictable. I could not close my diary with a more sobering thought for future fishing trips, whenever and wherever they may be.

Finale